Effective Writing:
A HANDBOOK FOR ACCOUNTANTS
SECOND EDITION

Claire Arevalo May
Communication Specialist
J. M. Tull School of Accounting
University of Georgia

PRENTICE HALL, Englewood Cliffs, New Jersey 07632

Library of Congress Cataloging-in-Publication Data

May, Claire Arevalo.
   Effective writing.

   Includes index.
    1. English language—Business
English. 2. Accounting—Language. I. Title.
PE1116.A3A8 1989   808'.066657   88–25500
ISBN 0–13–246539–6

Editorial/production supervision: Robert C. Walters
Interior design: Ann Lutz
Cover design: 20/20 Services, Inc.
Manufacturing buyer: Ed O'Dougherty

 ©1989, 1984 by Prentice-Hall, Inc.
A Division of Simon & Schuster
Englewood Cliffs, New Jersey 07632

Printed in the United States of America
10 9 8 7 6 5 4 3 2

ISBN 0-13-246539-6

Prentice-Hall International (UK) Limited, *London*
Prentice-Hall of Australia Pty. Limited, *Sydney*
Prentice-Hall Canada Inc., *Toronto*
Prentice-Hall Hispanoamericana, S.A., *Mexico City*
Prentice-Hall of India, Private Limited, *New Delhi*
Prentice-Hall of Japan, Inc., *Tokyo*
Prentice-Hall of Southeast Asia Pte. Ltd., *Singapore*
Editora Prentice-Hall do Brasil, Ltda, *Rio de Janeiro*

Contents

Preface

Effective Writing: A Handbook for Accountants, 2nd Edition, is designed to help accounting students and practitioners improve their writing skills. It can be used as a supplementary text for regular accounting courses, as a text in an accounting communication course, or as a text in a business communication or technical writing course when these courses include accounting students. The handbook is also a useful desk reference or self-study manual for accounting professionals.

Effective Writing guides the writer through all the stages of the writing process: planning, including analysis of audience and purpose; organizing the material; writing the draft; revising for readable style and correct grammar; and designing the document for effective presentation. In addition to these basic writing principles, the book includes chapters on letters, memos, reports, and other formats used by accountants in actual practice. Throughout all these chapters, *Effective Writing* stresses coherence, conciseness, and clarity as the most important qualities of the writing done by professional accountants.

Most chapters include exercises and writing topics for self-testing and practice. These assignments, like the illustrations in the text, deal with accounting concepts and situations, and thus will seem more relevant and interesting to men and women involved in the study and practice of accounting. Writing topics are keyed to the accounting courses for which they might be most suitable as class assignments.

One way to use *Effective Writing* is in conjunction with regular accounting courses. Instructors can assign cases and topics for research based on the accounting concepts actually being studied in class, or use the assignments provided in this handbook. Students then analyze the accounting problem, research the literature if necessary, and prepare their answers according to an assigned format such as a letter, technical memo, or formal report for a hypothetical client. The handbook will guide the students toward effective organization, style, format, grammar, and other elements of the writing process. Instructors can then evaluate the papers on the basis of accounting content and effective communication.

As a self-study manual, *Effective Writing* will help accounting professionals master the techniques of successful writing in the business world. The book contains numerous examples and practical applications of the techniques discussed. In addition, many chapters have exercises, with answers, which will enable the reader to practice the principles. A thoughtful review of *Effective Writing,* then, will give practicing accountants greater confidence in the writing situations that they encounter as part of their professional responsibilities.

The approaches to writing presented in this handbook have been used successfully at the J. M. Tull School of Accounting at the University of Georgia, which has pioneered in its writing program for accounting students.

The handbook covers the writing problems most frequently encountered by accounting students and practitioners, as demonstrated by extensive classroom testing and research into the communication needs of the profession. It is not intended to answer *all* questions of organization, style, or grammar, but it addresses the ones asked most frequently.

I wish to thank all the people who have helped me prepare this book:

- For helpful reviews of the manuscript: Professors Frances Teague, University of Georgia; Faye Borthick, University of Tennessee; William J. Radig, Marshall University; Mary Dehner, University of Georgia; and Gordon S. May, University of Georgia.
- For valuable suggestions on changes for the second edition: Professors Shirley Orechwa, University of Southern California; Brenda S. Birkett, Southern University; Catherine Begley, University of North Florida; Judith Cassidy, Louisiana State University; Helen M. Traugh, University of Alabama at Birmingham; Bob Keeny, Guilford College; and Tim Lockyer, DePaul University.
- For helping me prepare the manuscript: Evelyn S. Lapp, Anna Marie Soper, and Tammy Martin.

I also want to thank my family for their love and encouragement.

Claire Arevalo May

CHAPTER 1
Accountants As Writers

Most accountants are concerned about the need for effective writing skills. Multinational accounting firms offer special courses to help their accountants write better. Various accounting organizations—the AICPA and state societies, for example—offer continuing professional education courses in writing. Many colleges and universities now stress effective writing in accounting coursework.

Why all this interest in writing? To be truly competent, accountants must be able to use words effectively. In a study published by the AICPA, Robert H. Roy and James H. MacNeill stressed the importance of effective accounting communication:

> To [CPAs] the ability to express [themselves] well is more than the hallmark of educated [persons]; it is a professional necessity. Inability to express [their] findings in understandable, explicit, unambiguous, intelligible English can be self-defeating, potentially misleading, and possibly disastrous to clients, creditors, and investors. ...We feel justified, therefore...in being unequivocal about this requirement of the common body of knowledge for beginning CPAs: *candidates who cannot write the English language at least as well as a minimum-threshold should be denied admission to the profession, if need be on this account alone.*[1]

The American Accounting Association's Committee to Prepare a Statement of Basic Accounting Theory also identified the importance of communication in the practice of accounting: "Communication is a vital link in accounting activity. It is of no less importance than that of developing the information itself."[2]

So the ability to communicate effectively—whether in speaking or writing—is essential to success in the accounting profession.

Unfortunately, many students and accountants lack the basic skills they need to be effective communicators. *The Wall Street Journal* recently reported that as many as one-third of the accounting firms surveyed are dissatisfied with the communication skills of entry-level accountants.[3] In another study to determine why entry-level accountants lose their jobs, a high percentage of firms reported poor writing skills as a major reason for job terminations.[4]

Because the ability to communicate effectively plays an important part in an accountant's success on the job, employers have started to screen prospective accountants for adequate skills in oral and written communication. In fact, one study shows communication skills to be the most important factor in decisions to hire new accountants. Employers view the ability to write and speak effectively as even more important than a prospective employee's grade point average.[5]

So accountants need good communication skills to get a good job in the first place, and to keep that job after they are hired. Of course "communication skills" is a broad area. It includes formal and informal oral presentations, interpersonal communication, nonverbal communication, and many other areas as well. But since this is a book about writing, let us look further at some of the kinds of documents accountants write on the job.

WHAT DO ACCOUNTANTS WRITE?

No matter what kind of practice accountants have, writing is an essential part of the job. Whether in public accounting, management accounting, not-for-profit accounting, or governmental accounting, and whether specializing in tax, auditing, systems, or some other area, accountants write every day.

Examples in three areas, tax, auditing, and systems, will suggest a few of the many occasions that require accountants to write. A tax accountant often writes memos to describe to other members of the firm the results of his or her research. These memos often become part of the clients' files. Then the accountant may write a letter to the clients advising them about the best way to handle the tax problem. Often tax accountants must also write letters to the Internal Revenue Service on behalf of clients.

Auditors write memos to be filed with the audit working papers describing the work done on an audit. Auditors may also write memos to their colleagues to request advice or to report research results. Following the audit engagement, auditors often write advisory letters to management of the audited firm; the purpose of these letters is to suggest ways to improve accounting and internal control procedures.

Systems specialists might write documents for readers with varying degrees of computer expertise. For example, they might write a user primer to explain in elementary terms how to use a certain software package. Or they might write a highly technical report on a complex accounting system application.

No matter what their specialty, all accountants write memos to their supervisors, subordinates, and co-workers to request information or to give it. They also write letters to clients, agencies, and a variety of other readers.

Reports, both formal and informal, are also important ways accountants communicate. For instance, an accountant working for a corporation may write a report for management on alternative accounting treatments for a particular kind of business transaction.

To be effective, letters, memos, and reports must be well written. How will clients react if, after reading a letter from their CPA, they are still confused about their income tax problem? How will management feel about a report that is poorly organized and hard to follow?

Yet another kind of writing prepared by some accountants is the narrative portions of financial statements. For instance, footnote disclosures communicate information that users may need to interpret the statements accurately. Here is an example of a footnote disclosure in the 1985 annual report of the Maytag Company:[6]

SHAREOWNERS' EQUITY

During 1985 the Company amended its Articles of Incorporation to increase the number of authorized shares of Common stock from 20,000,000 to 100,000,000 and to authorize a new class of 12,000,000 shares of Preferred stock with a $1 par value.

On December 27, 1985 the shareowners approved a two-for-one Common stock split and a change in par value from $2.50 to $1.25. In the accompanying financial statements and notes the number of shares and per share amounts have been restated to give retroactive effect to the stock split.

This footnote is fairly easy to understand. Unfortunately, the meaning of some footnote disclosures is not always clear to the average financial statement reader. Arthur Adelberg and Richard Lewis, in an article in the *Journal of Accountancy,* note the need for more clearly written footnotes. They suggest, for instance, that accountants use shorter sentences, active verbs, and definitions of technical terms when writing footnotes and other narrative portions of financial statements.[7]*

HOW WELL DO ACCOUNTANTS WRITE?

The answer to this question—how well do accountants write—has already been suggested by the study reporting the large numbers of entry-level accountants who lose their jobs because of poor writing skills. And some employers believe the problem is getting worse. One study suggests that almost half of all Big Eight practitioners believe that writing skills of their newly hired staff have declined in the last few years.[8]

*Copyright © 1980 by the American Institute of Certified Public Accountants.

A letter to *The Wall Street Journal* points out the high costs to employers when their employees lack adequate writing skills, including the costs of quality control measures to correct faulty writing. In addition, "The expense of hiring and training those who are subsequently fired for [poor writing ability] must surely represent a tremendous waste of resources."[9]

In a study sponsored by the American Accounting Association, Robert W. Ingram and Charles R. Frazier identified 20 communication skills important to the successful practice of accounting. A disturbing finding of the study was that *entry-level staff and accounting students are woefully deficient in most of these skills.*[10]

Of the skills identified by Ingram and Frazier, the following relate directly or indirectly to effective writing:[11]

- correspondence writing
- memorandums and informal report writing
- formal report writing
- correct grammar
- correct punctuation
- correct spelling
- outline development
- inductive reasoning
- deductive reasoning
- coherence
- clarity
- conciseness
- paragraph development
- use of visual aids

It is the purpose of this book to help those preparing to enter the accounting profession and those already in the profession to improve on these very important writing skills.

WHAT MAKES WRITING WORK?

Ingram and Frazier's list of writing skills suggests some of the qualities of effective writing. Three of these qualities, coherence, clarity, and conciseness, summarize the others on the list.

Coherence is the logical, orderly relationship of ideas. Coherent writing is, quite simply, writing that is well organized. The flow of thought is easy to follow and important ideas stand out. For a document to be coherent, the writer must carefully think through the ideas he or she wishes to convey. The ideas must be arranged logically, and then written in a way readers will be able to comprehend.

Clarity means that the writing is written as simply as possible, using words and phrases with which the reader is familiar. Words are chosen to mean precisely what the writer intended, and sentences convey only one meaning: the meaning the writer meant to convey. Correct grammar, punctuation, and spelling also contribute to clear writing.

Conciseness means that a writer says what needs to be said in as few words as possible. To keep their writing concise, good writers avoid digressions, unnecessary repetition, and a wordy style.

Coherence, clarity, and conciseness: these are the qualities of effective writing, the qualities that make writing work.

In conclusion, it is important to remember that accounting is a process of measuring and *communicating* information. Accountants need writing skills for many of their routine, professional tasks, whether communicating with investors, management, clients, or fellow professionals. They need to use words effectively and to combine these words into good sentences and paragraphs.

Writing skills pay off in professional advancement. Zane Robbins, of Arthur Andersen & Co., notes:

> All other things being equal, the professional accountant who can communicate best is likely to progress fastest. Those who are unable to write and communicate effectively often find themselves consigned to the purgatory of technician with little hope for long-term growth.[12]

To succeed professionally, accountants must master many skills. They must understand and be able to apply accounting principles, of course, but they must also be able to communicate effectively. A competent accountant who is also an effective writer will usually be rewarded with professional success.

EXERCISES

Exercise 1-1

Look for examples of effective and ineffective writing in the material you read regularly. Consider letters and memos you receive, as well as published professional material such as textbooks, professional articles, and FASB pronouncements. Then think about the following questions.

1. What kind of material do you find easiest to read? What are some of the qualities that make this writing readable?
2. Examine closely the writing you find difficult to read. How do you think the writing could be improved?

3.   Make two lists of the specific qualities that make writing effective or ineffective. You might begin with these qualities:

EFFECTIVE WRITING	INEFFECTIVE WRITING
• conversational, everyday vocabulary	• jargon and ''big words''
• main ideas easy to identify; gets to the point	• rambling, unorganized; fails to get to the point quickly
• correct grammar and spelling	• obvious grammatical and spelling mistakes
• short paragraphs	• long paragraphs
• concise	• longer than it needs to be
• etc.	• etc.

Exercise 1-2

Collect samples of your own writing. Analyze your writing, considering the following questions.

1.   What kind of response do you usually get to your writing from your supervisors, peers, clients, and subordinates? Are readers sometimes uncertain of your meaning?
2.   From the lists you made for Exercise 1-1, question 3, identify some of the strengths and weaknesses of your writing.

NOTES

1. Robert H. Roy and James H. MacNeill, *Horizons for a Profession: The Common Body of Knowledge for Certified Public Accountants* (New York: American Institute of Certified Public Accountants, 1967), pp. 218–19.
2. Committee to Prepare a Statement of Basic Accounting Theory, *A Statement of Basic Accounting Theory* (Evanston, Ill.: American Accounting Association, 1966), p. 13.
3. ''Words Count,'' *Wall Street Journal,* July 16, 1986, p. 1.
4. Alan A. Cherry and Lucy A. Wilson, ''A Study of the Writing Skills of Accounting Majors in California'' (unpublished study, 1987).
5. ''Popularity Poll Results,'' *New Accountant,* September 1986, p. 20.
6. The Maytag Company, ''Notes to Consolidated Financial Statements,'' *1985 Annual Report.*
7. Arthur Harris Adelberg and Richard A. Lewis, ''Financial Reports Can Be Made More Understandable,'' *Journal of Accountancy,* 149 (June 1980): 44–50.
8. Daniel P. Murphy, ''An Analysis of the Application Skills Needed by Undergraduate Accounting Students Planning to Enter Tax Practice in the Southeastern United States: A Practitioner's Perspective,'' *Collected Papers of the American Accounting Association's Southeast Regional Meeting* (Atlanta: n.p., 1987), p. 120.
9. Gordon S. May, ''No Accounting for Poor Writers,'' *Wall Street Journal,* Letter to the Editor, May 29, 1987, p. 27.
10. Robert W. Ingram and Charles R. Frazier, *Developing Communications Skills for the Accounting Profession* (Evanston, Ill.: American Accounting Association, 1980).
11. Ibid., pp. 15–18.
12. H. Zane Robbins, ''How to Develop Basic Writing Skills,'' *The Chronicle,* 40, no. 1 (1981), 9.

CHAPTER 2
The Writing Process:
An Overview

Effective writing, like accounting, is a process. The first step in the accounting process is to analyze the transactions to determine how they should be recorded. For example, the accountant decides where to record the transactions—what journals, ledgers, and accounts to use—and how detailed the entry description must be in order to be useful.

Several questions basic to the accounting system underlie an accountant's analysis of financial transactions and their treatment. What is the purpose of the information recorded and ultimately reported? Who are the users of this information and what are their needs? How can this information be most fairly and effectively presented?

These questions are as important to good writing as they are to good accounting. Initial planning, emphasizing both the purpose of the writing and the needs of the readers, is the first step in the writing process.

This chapter will discuss the writing process from beginning to end: planning for purpose and audience, generating and organizing ideas, drafting, revising, and proofreading. It will then show you how to apply this process to solve the problem of writer's block. Finally, the chapter will show how word processors can help you at every stage of the writing process.

GETTING STARTED:
ANALYZING THE PURPOSE

The first stage in the writing process, analyzing the purpose of what you are to write, is often overlooked. When you think about purpose, you decide what you want to accomplish with your letter, memo, or other document. Do you want to provide your readers with information about some topic, answer their questions, recommend a course of action? Persuade them to do something or agree with you on some point?

These are just a few of the purposes a document can have. What is important, however, is that you think carefully about the purpose *before* you begin to write. It might be helpful to think of purpose in terms of three categories: to give information about something, to propose a course of action, or to solve a problem. The purpose of most writing tasks will fall into one of these categories, or perhaps a combination of two or three.

A report on inventory flow assumptions, for example, could have numerous purposes. If you were writing such a report, you would first decide on its primary purpose. Should the report simply describe the various flow assumptions—LIFO, FIFO, average cost, etc.? Is the purpose of the report to recommend an inventory accounting treatment for a certain company in a given situation? Should the report analyze the potential problems arising from a change in flow assumptions—from FIFO to LIFO, perhaps?

Here is another example. Assume you are the controller for Eldorado Manufacturing. Eldorado is considering a purchase of stock from Western Materials, one of Eldorado's major suppliers of raw materials. A report on this possible purchase could have any of the following purposes:

- To inform management of the advantages (or disadvantages) of such a purchase
- To recommend that Eldorado purchase (or not purchase) the stock
- To suggest a way to finance the purchase

The purpose of the report, or of any writing, will determine what material it should contain. Consider another example. Your client is faced with a lawsuit that could result in a large loss. You might write a report for the client about the disclosure requirements for contingent loss liabilities due to pending litigation. In such a report you would not include a discussion of gain contingencies, nor a discussion of loss contingencies from bad debts. You would analyze the specific purpose of the report to decide what information was relevant for this situation.

It is a good idea to write down the purpose of your writing task before you begin further work on it. Be as specific as possible, and try to define your purpose within one sentence. This sentence may later become part of the introduction of your letter, memo, or report.

Two final words about purpose: *be specific.* Remember that you are writing to particular individuals in a particular situation. Relate the purpose of your writing to these people and their concerns. In the Eldorado Manufacturing example, suppose you were writing a report on how to finance a purchase of Western Materials stock. You would limit your discussion to the financing alternatives available to Eldorado and those practical for it to consider.

ANALYZING THE READERS

Another important consideration in the planning of a writing task is who the reader(s) will be. A report on a highly technical accounting topic would be written one way for a fellow accountant, but another way for a client with only limited knowledge of accounting procedures and terminology.

Effective writers analyze the needs of their readers. If you are writing a report, letter, or memo, you will likely be writing to a limited number of people, or perhaps for only one person. Furthermore, you usually know, or can find out, important information about the readers. Again, you must ask certain basic questions. How much knowledge do the readers have of the subject being discussed? The answer to this question will determine the terms that should be defined, the procedures that should be explained, or the background information that should be provided.

Accountants dealing with the public should be particularly careful in analyzing the needs of their readers. For example, a tax specialist might have clients with widely varying experience and knowledge of taxation terminology. A corporation executive would probably understand such concepts as deferrals and loss carryforwards. But a small shopkeeper might not be familiar with these technical accounting terms and procedures. Business letters to these two clients, even on the same topic, would need to be written differently.

You should also consider the readers' attitudes and biases. Are they likely to be neutral to your recommendations, or will they need to be convinced? Remember to write with the readers' interests and needs in mind. How will the readers benefit, directly or indirectly, from what you propose? How can you present your arguments so that readers' objections and biases will be overcome? To answer this last question you will need to anticipate readers' questions, research the basic issues, and then organize your arguments into a convincing arrangement (see the following section).

Other important considerations when analyzing readers' needs are tone and style. Again, what are their attitudes and biases? Some readers react well to an informal, friendly style of writing, but other readers believe that professional writing should be more formal. Chapter 4 discusses tone and style in more detail.

Consider also your word choices. Would some of your readers resent the following sentence?

> An efficient accountant dictates letters to his secretary; she then types the letters for his signature.

Some readers might argue that the choice of pronouns (accountant/he, secretary/she) implies a sexist bias. More traditional readers might not object to the sentence at all. (Note: this sentence can be revised to avoid the issue of sexism by using plural nouns: Efficient accountants dictate letters to their secretaries, who then type the letters for their supervisors' signatures.)

But whoever your reader is, remember always to be courteous. Whether you write in a technical or simplified style, all readers appreciate (and deserve!) consideration, tact, and respect.

Analyzing reader needs is an important part of the preparation for writing. Initial planning, which considers both your audience and your purpose, is the first rule of effective writing:

1. **Analyze the purpose of the writing and the needs of the readers.**

GETTING YOUR IDEAS TOGETHER

Once you have evaluated the purpose of the writing and the needs of the readers, you are ready for the second stage in the writing process: organizing the ideas you want to present. This step may be quick and simple. For a short letter you can list the three or four ideas you wish to include in the letter, perhaps one idea for each paragraph.

For a longer piece of writing, getting your ideas together may be a more complicated process, one involving a great deal of thought on your part, and perhaps some research as well.

The place to start, though, is the work you have already done. Because you have identified the purposes of your writing and the needs and interests of your reader, you already have the skeleton of an outline. You know the most important topics you need to cover, and you also have an idea of the best approach to use for presenting those ideas. In other words, you have a focus for your writing.

If you have not already written your statement of purpose, now is the time to do so. Try to break the purpose up into several subtopics. For example, suppose the purpose of a letter to a client is to recommend that the client expand her computerized accounting system. The statement of purpose for this letter could specify the different accounting jobs for which the expanded system would be useful, or outline the major advantages of the system.

Another useful technique for generating ideas is brainstorming. With this technique, you think about your topic and write down all the ideas that come to you, in whatever order they come. You do not worry about organizing the ideas, nor do you evaluate them. Just write them down. Later you can consider how, and if, these ideas fit into the skeletal outline that you developed when you analyzed the purposes of the document you are writing.

In some situations, you may need to do some background reading or research before you can develop your outline further. If you are writing a research report on a technical topic, for example, you may need to survey the literature to identify the important aspects of the subject; these aspects will then become the major divisions of the outline. Chapter 11 discusses background reading, as well as other phases of the research process, in more detail.

Most outlines are organized in a complex-deductive structure: a main idea, major supporting ideas, and minor supporting ideas. Chapters 3 and 10 contain further discussion of complex-deductive patterns of organization.

After you have made a list or outline of your important ideas, you can consider several questions. Does the outline cover the subject completely, or should you expand it to include other ideas? Does it include a topic that is not relevant to the purpose of the writing? Have you presented the ideas in the most effective order?

The order in which you present your ideas is an important consideration. To some extent the order will depend on the particular document you are writing. However, several principles of good organization apply to all writing tasks.

First, nearly all writing has the same basic structure:

> *Introduction:* identifies the subject of the document and tells why it was written. Sometimes the introduction also provides background information about the topic or stresses its importance.
>
> *Concise statement of the main ideas:* summarizes explicitly your main ideas, conclusions, or recommendations. This part of a document may be part of the introduction or a separate section. It can be as short as a one-sentence statement of purpose, or as long as a three-page executive summary in a report.
>
> *Development of the main ideas:* includes explanations, examples, analyses, steps, reasons, proofs. This part of an outline or paper is often called the body.
>
> *Conclusion:* brings the paper to an effective close. The conclusion may restate the main idea in a fresh way, suggest further work, or summarize recommendations. An effective conclusion will not include unnecessary repetition, however.

Later chapters of this handbook will discuss more fully this basic structure as it is used for particular kinds of writing.

Another principle of effective organization is to arrange the ideas in a logical order. For instance, if you were describing the process of reconciling bank statements, you would discuss each step of the procedure in the order in which it is performed.

Finally, you can often organize ideas according to their importance. In business writing, always arrange your ideas from the most to the least important.

Remember, business documents are not like detective stories. You do not save the best for last, nor do you keep your readers in suspense about your conclusions.

Suppose you are writing a report to recommend that your firm purchase a new computer system for its accounting records. Naturally, you will want to emphasize the advantages of this purchase—describing them in the order that is likely to be most convincing *to the readers* of the report. However, an investment in a computerized accounting system might also have drawbacks—for example, the cost to purchase and install the equipment and the problems involved in converting to the new system. For your report to appear well researched and unbiased, you will need to include these disadvantages in your discussion—and, of course, in the outline as you are preparing the report. To organize your report, you might use the following basic structure:

I. Introduction, including your recommendation
II. Body
    A. Advantages, beginning with those most appealing to the readers
    B. Disadvantages, including, when possible, ways to minimize or overcome any drawbacks
III. Conclusion

If you analyze your outline or list of ideas before you begin to write, you will be able to decide in advance how to present your thoughts most effectively. You will also know that you have covered the subject thoroughly, but eliminated unnecessary digressions. This time spent in organizing the writing task will save time and effort when you actually begin to write. By following the outline, you will always know what to say next.

The list of rules for effective writing can now be expanded:

1. **Analyze the purpose of the writing and the needs of the readers.**
2. **Use an outline to organize the ideas you want to present.**

WRITING THE DRAFT

The third step in the writing process is the draft. The purpose of this step is to get the ideas down on paper in whatever form they come most easily. Spelling, punctuation, and style are not important in the draft. What is important is to write the ideas down so that later you can polish and correct them.

When you work on your draft, follow the outline you have already prepared. However, you may decide to change the outline as you go, omitting some parts that no longer seem to fit, or adding other ideas that now seem necessary. Changing the outline is fine, because when you revise the draft later you can make sure your thoughts are still well organized.

While you will use your outline as a guide to the ideas you want to include in your draft, you may find it easier to write the various parts of the document in a different order from the one in the outline. Some people find introductions hard to write, so they leave them until last. You may also choose to write the easiest sections of your draft first, or you may start writing some parts of the draft while you are still getting the material together for other parts.

One final word of advice on the draft stage: do not allow yourself to get stuck while you search for the perfect word, phrase, or sentence. Leave a blank space or write something that is more-or-less what you mean. You will probably be able to find the right words later when you revise the draft.

REVISING THE DRAFT

The next stage in the writing process is the revision of the draft. It is in this stage that you check your spelling and grammar and polish your style. Make a final check also to see that the ideas are effectively and completely presented.

You will need to revise most of your writing more than once—perhaps even three or four times. The key to revising is to let the writing get cold between revisions; a time lapse between readings will enable you to read more objectively what you have written—what you have actually said, instead of what you meant to say. Ideally, revisions should be at least a day apart.

The next four chapters of the handbook will discuss what to look for when putting your writing in final form.

We now have three rules for effective writing:

1. **Analyze the purpose of the writing and the needs of the readers.**
2. **Use an outline to organize the ideas you want to present.**
3. **Write the draft, and then revise it to make the writing polished and correct.**

THE FINAL DRAFT

After you have polished the style and organization of the paper, you will be ready to put it in its final form. It is important to consider questions of document design, such as the use of headings, white space, and other elements of the paper's appearance. Chapter 6 discusses these topics in some detail.

Proofreading is also an important step when you put your paper in its final form. Here are some suggestions for effective proofreading:

1. Proofreading will usually be easier if you leave some time between typing and looking for errors. You will see the paper more clearly if you have been away from it for awhile.
2. If possible, use a word processor with a spelling check program to eliminate spelling and typographical errors.
3. If you do not have access to a word processor, use a dictionary to look up any word that could possibly be misspelled. If you are a poor speller, you might have someone else read your paper for spelling errors.
4. If you know you have a tendency to make a certain type of error, read through your paper at least once with the specific purpose of checking for that error. For example, if you have problems with verb agreement (see Chapter 5), check every sentence in your paper to be sure the verbs are correct.

5. Read your paper backwards, sentence by sentence, as a final proofreading step. This technique will isolate each sentence and should make it easier to spot errors you may have overlooked in previous readings.

DEALING WITH WRITER'S BLOCK

Writer's block is a problem all of us face at some time or another. This problem occurs when we stare at blank paper or at a blank screen with no idea of how to get started on the writing task. The ideas and the words just don't come.

Many of the techniques already discussed in this chapter will help you overcome writer's block. In the first place, thinking of writing as a process, rather than a completed product that appears suddenly in its final form, should help make the job less formidable. Any difficult task seems easier if you break it down into manageable steps.

The discussions of the steps in the writing process, especially the section on writing the draft, have included suggestions that will help you overcome writer's block. Here is a summary of these techniques:

1. Plan before you write, so that you know what you need to say.
2. Write with an outline in view, but do not be tied to it. Write the paper in any order you wish; you can rearrange it later.
3. Do not strive for perfection in the draft stage. Leave problems of grammar, spelling, style, and so forth to the revision stage.
4. Begin with the easiest sections to write.
5. Do not get stuck on difficult places. Skip over them and go on to something else. You may find that when you come back to the rough spots later they will not be as hard to write as you had thought at first.

WORD PROCESSING

Many writers find that word processing helps with writer's block and many other writing problems as well. If you have not already learned to use a good word processing program, by all means become proficient in using one.

It is beyond the scope of this book to discuss specific word processing programs or to give instructions for their use. But we should mention a few of the ways typical programs can help you with your writing.

Writers who are proficient at word processing believe they are a big help at every stage of the writing process, from planning through proofreading. Perhaps a word processor is most helpful, however, at the revision stage. With the help of a few simple commands, you can add text, delete it, or rearrange it. You can insert sentences, change your wording, and move paragraphs around. You can make minor changes to your draft or major ones, all the time preserving the remainder of the draft without retyping.

Many word processing programs also come with a spelling checker for identifying misspelled words and typographical errors. A spelling checker is nearly indispensible for those of us who have reached adulthood without really learning how to spell, since we do not want to embarrass ourselves by leaving spelling errors in the final draft. But a word of warning is in order: word processors do not catch errors in the use of homonyms, like their/there, affect/effect, or its/it's.

Some writers are so enthusiastic about word processing that they claim a whole new world of writing ease has opened up to them with the help of this technology. This claim may be an exaggeration, because word processors cannot tell you what to write. Once you know what you want to say, however, they make the mechanics of writing and rewriting a much easier job.

EXERCISES

Exercise 2-1

Among your business correspondents are the following people:

1. The controller of a large corporation—a fellow accountant.
2. A manager in a large corporation—educated and experienced in business, though not an accountant.
3. The owner/president of a medium-sized business (2,500 employees)—experienced in business, but with little formal education.
4. The new owner of a small business—little business education or experience.
5. Stockholders of a large corporation.
6. A bookkeeper under your supervision.

For each correspondent, which of the following terms or procedures would you *likely* need to explain?

a. GAAP
b. FASB
c. LIFO
d. historical cost
e. lower of cost or market
f. earnings statement
g. owners' equity
h. quick ratio
i. accounts receivable
j. rent expense
k. double-entry bookkeeping
l. capital leases—accounting for lessee

Exercise 2-2

You have been hired as a special assistant to Sam Jones, the president of Bulldog Sales Company. Mr. Jones has little formal education, but is very astute about business matters and is an especially good salesperson. He calls you in and says, "Bulldog Sales Company is in the nice position of having excess cash on hand. I am considering investing that cash in some bonds issued five years ago by Red and Black Company, but I see in *The Wall Street Journal* that those bonds are selling at only 60 percent of their maturity value. Does that mean they are especially risky? Assuming I do make this investment, what are the accounting implications? Write a memo to me that will answer these questions."[1]

Analyze the purpose of the memo that you will write to Mr. Jones. What topics should you include to answer his questions? Are the following topics relevant to the purpose of the memo? Why?

definition of a bond
reasons for investing excess cash
bond discounts: what they mean
bond premiums: what they mean
accounting for bond premiums
accounting for bond discounts

Exercise 2-3

You are the newest member of the accounting staff of Monroe Sales Company. The president of the company, Susan Monroe, has just learned that the accounting department uses a general journal and four special journals.

Ms. Monroe does not understand why the accounting department uses five journals. She believes it would save time and decrease the chance of errors if only one journal were used. She asks you to write a memo in response to her suggestion.

1. What is the purpose of this memo? What topics should you include in the memo so that it will accomplish this purpose?
2. What should you consider when you analyze the reader of your memo?

Exercise 2-4

The society of CPAs in your state is offering a continuing professional education seminar entitled "Effective Writing." You want your firm to give you released time to attend the seminar and you would like to have your expenses paid. Your supervisor, Carol Black, is unfamiliar with the seminar; you will need to convince her that your attendance would benefit the firm by making you a more effective employee. You need to write a memo to Ms. Black explaining your request.[2]

1. What ideas and information should you include in the memo?

2. How could you arrange this information in an effective order? Write an outline; be careful to include all relevant details about the seminar and an adequate justification for your request.

ANSWERS TO EXERCISES

Answers, Exercise 2-1

1. 1
2. a–e, h, 1
3. a–e, g, h, k, l
4. a–1
5. a–e, h, k, l
6. a–c, e, h, l

Answers, Exercise 2-2

These topics would be relevant to Mr. Jones's questions about the Red and Black bonds:

bond discounts: what they mean
accounting for bond discounts

Note: You might need to include other topics in your memo, as well. For example, you might want to list other accounting implications of bond investments. And you should specifically answer Mr. Jones's question about the riskiness of the Red and Black bonds. You might include a brief discussion of risk when you explain bond discounts.

Answers, Exercise 2-3

1. The purpose of the memo will be to convince Ms. Monroe that the use of five journals is beneficial to her company. Thus the purpose is partly to inform: what the journals are, how they are used, and how they help Monroe Sales Company run more efficiently. The purpose of the memo is also to persuade Ms. Monroe that the accounting staff should continue its use of all five journals.

    The memo might identify the journals and briefly describe the purposes of each. It would then discuss advantages to the Monroe Sales Company of using the journals. You would need to be very specific about these advantages as they relate to Monroe Sales. For example, one benefit is that special journals simplify posting to the ledger. To illustrate this point, you could mention how Monroe's bookkeepers are able to post column totals rather than individual transactions.

2. One concern in analyzing the reader of this memo is to decide what Ms. Monroe would need to have explained or defined. You know, because she does not understand the need for the five journals, that she has very little knowledge of accounting. Thus she would not understand what you meant by the adjusting and closing entries that

go into the general journal. On the other hand, she would know that her customers often purchase goods on credit, so you would not need to explain credit sales when you discuss the sales journal.

The question of tone is very important with this memo. It is always a tricky matter to tell the boss she is wrong, so you will need to be tactful and diplomatic. On the other hand, you do not want to sound condescending because you have to explain something that to you is very elementary. You do not want to talk down to Ms. Monroe; as always, you want to be respectful, courteous, and helpful.

Answer, Exercise 2–4

Possible outline:

I. Introduction
  A. Identify the seminar
  B. Make a specific request
II. The seminar
  A. Where
  B. When
  C. Sponsorship
  D. Cost of seminar, including registration, travel, and living expenses.
  Note: You may have already provided some of this information for I.A. above. Don't repeat yourself.
III. Why you should go. These reasons will vary. For example, the seminar should improve your writing in several ways:
  A. Instructions to subordinates
  B. Reports and proposals to supervisors
  C. Letters and reports to clients
IV. Conclusion

NOTES

1. Gadis J. Dillon, "Writing Assignment for Intermediate Accounting" (unpublished class assignment, University of Georgia, 1982).
2. Ibid.

CHAPTER 3
The Flow of Thought: Organizing for Coherence

In Chapter 1 we identified coherence as one of the three most important qualities of business writing. Coherent writing is organized so that important ideas stand out; the flow of thought is logical and easy to follow.

Chapter 2 introduced some important techniques for achieving coherence: analyzing your purpose and the reader's needs, and then planning and outlining before you begin to write. This chapter will discuss additional ways to make your writing coherent. It will discuss how to write with unity, use summary sentences and transitions, and organize effective paragraphs.

WRITING WITH UNITY

The key to unified writing is to establish the main idea of each writing task. An office memo may contain only one paragraph, but that paragraph will have a central idea. A report may run to many pages, but it will still have a central idea or purpose, and possibly secondary purposes as well. It is important to decide on your main ideas before you begin writing, preferably before you begin your outline. Deciding on the main idea for a writing task is similar to analyzing its purpose, as we discussed in Chapter 2.

You should be able to summarize a main idea in one sentence. In a paragraph, this sentence is called the topic sentence. In longer writings involving more than two or three paragraphs, this sentence may be called the thesis statement or a statement of purpose.

The main idea is the key to the entire writing task. Every other sentence should be related to it, either directly or indirectly. The central idea is like the hub of a wheel or the trunk of a tree. All other ideas branch off from the central idea; they explain it, analyze it, illustrate it, or prove it. Any sentences or details that are unrelated to the main idea, either directly or indirectly, are irrelevant (off the subject) and should be omitted. In longer writings, entire paragraphs may be irrelevant to the main purpose; these irrelevant paragraphs are called digressions.

When you remove digressions and irrelevant sentences, you achieve unified writing: every sentence, either directly or indirectly, is related to the main idea.

The paragraph below is not unified. Which sentences do you think are irrelevant to the topic sentence?

> (1) Incorporation offers many advantages for a business and its owners. (2) For example, the owners are not responsible for the business's debts. (3) Investors hope to make money when they buy stock in a corporation. (4) Incorporation also enables a business to obtain professional management skills. (5) Corporations are subject to more government regulation than are other forms of organization.

Sentence 1, the topic sentence, identifies what should be the main idea of the paragraph: the advantages of incorporation. Sentences 3 and 5 are off the subject.

Writing with unity is an important way to make your writing coherent.

USING SUMMARY SENTENCES

Another characteristic of coherent writing is that the main ideas stand out. You can emphasize your main ideas by placing them in the document where they will get the reader's attention.

First, as Chapter 2 suggested, it is important to summarize all of your main ideas at the beginning of your document. For a short document, especially a report, you will need a separate summary section at or near the beginning of the paper. This formal summary may be called an abstract, executive summary, or simply the summary.

When writing these summary sections, be specific and remember your reader's interests and needs. Let us say you are writing a memo to the president of Monroe Sales Company to explain the advantages of using special journals. Do not be satisfied with writing something vague, like "There are many advantages of using special journals." Summarize those advantages specifically, and relate them to Monroe Sales Company. For example, one of the advantages might be "Special journals save our accounting staff time when we post totals to the ledger."

The summary at the beginning of a paper may be several sentences or even pages long, depending on the length of the paper and the complexity of your main ideas or recommendations. Here is an example:

> ABC Company should establish the following procedures to ensure a smooth transition to its new computerized system:

- Management should designate a representative from each department to attend the three-week workshop at company headquarters.
- Each department should plan a training session for its employees to emphasize the department's use of the system.
- A two-month transition period should be allowed for converting from the old system.
- EDP trouble-shooters should be available to all departments to solve any problems that occur.

Summary sentences are important in other places besides the beginning of a document. They are also important to begin each section of the paper and as part of the conclusion.

Any paper that is longer than three or four paragraphs probably has more than one main idea and/or recommendation; each of these ideas is, of course, stated in the introduction or in a separate summary section. Often the logical way to organize the remainder of the document is to use a separate section of the paper to discuss each idea further. Each section would then begin with a summary statement to identify the main idea, or the topic, of that section. The reader will then have a clear idea of what that section is about. It is a good idea, of course, to use somewhat different wording from that used in the beginning of the paper.

Finally, summary statements are also important in the conclusions of many documents, especially if the paper is very long. Once again, you may need to remind the reader of your main ideas. However, you need to be careful not to sound repetitive, so you will have to be guided by the length and complexity of your document in deciding how much detail to include in your conclusion section. Later chapters of this book discuss conclusions further.

PARAGRAPHS

In addition to improving the coherence of the entire document, summary statements also contribute to coherent paragraphs. The sentence that summarizes the main idea of a paragraph is called its topic sentence. In business writing it is usually a good idea to begin each paragraph with a topic sentence.

This section of the chapter will be devoted to techniques of paragraphing: how to plan length, structure, and development so that your paragraphs contribute to coherent writing.

Length

Some writers are not always sure how long paragraphs should be. Are one-sentence paragraphs acceptable? What about paragraphs that run on for nearly an entire typed page?

One rule is that a paragraph should be limited to the development of one idea. Thus, the length of most paragraphs is somewhere between one sentence and an entire page. However, an occasional short paragraph, even of only one sentence, may be effective to emphasize an idea or to provide a transition between two major divisions of the writing.

Effective writers, remembering the needs of their readers, will be wary of long paragraphs, which look intimidating and are often hard to follow. You may need to divide a long paragraph into two shorter ones. Appropriate transitions can tie the two paragraphs together and maintain a smooth flow of thought.

A good rule of thumb is to limit most of your paragraphs to four or five sentences.

Structure

Another feature of well-written paragraphs is their structure. We have already suggested that a strong topic sentence can contribute to a unified, coherent paragraph. A topic sentence states the main idea of the paragraph. It is usually the first sentence in the paragraph, and sometimes it contains a transition tying the new paragraph to the previous one. All other sentences in the paragraph should develop the idea expressed in the topic sentence.

Two patterns of paragraph organization are useful for accountants' writing tasks—the simple-deductive paragraph and the complex-deductive paragraph. The simple-deductive arrangement states the main idea in the first sentence (topic sentence); all other sentences *directly* develop that idea through explanation, illustration, or analysis. A concluding sentence is sometimes helpful. Here is an example of a simple-deductive paragraph:

(1) Accountants never finish their educations. (2) They work hard for their college degrees, but after college they must continue studying to stay current on the latest developments in the profession. (3) They must be thoroughly familiar with changing governmental regulations and new pronouncements by professional organizations like the FASB. (4) To improve their professional competence, they participate in a variety of continuing education programs sponsored by such organizations as the AICPA and state accounting societies. (5) Indeed, well-qualified accountants will be lifetime students, always seeking better ways to serve their clients and the public.

In this paragraph, sentence 1 is the topic sentence, sentences 2–4 develop the main idea, and sentence 5 is the conclusion. A simple-deductive paragraph has a simple structural diagram:

(1) Topic sentence—main idea
  (2) Supporting sentence
  (3) Supporting sentence
  (4) Supporting sentence
(5) Concluding sentence (optional)

A complex-deductive paragraph has a more elaborate structure. This paragraph is complex-deductive:

(1) Financial statements are important to a variety of users. (2) First, investors and potential investors use the statements to decide if a company is a good investment risk. (3) These users look at such factors as net income, the debt-to-equity ratio, and retained earnings. (4) Second, creditors use financial statements to decide if a firm is a good credit risk. (5) Creditors want to know if a firm has a large enough cash flow to pay its debts. (6) Third, governmental agencies analyze financial statements for a variety of purposes. (7) For example, the Internal Revenue Service will want to know if the company has paid the required amount of taxes on its income. (8) These examples of financial statement users show how diverse their interests can be.

In this paragraph, sentence 1 (topic sentence) states the main idea. Sentence 2 directly supports the main idea by giving an example of it, but sentence 3 explains sentence 2. Thus sentence 3 directly supports sentence 2, but only indirectly supports sentence 1. Complex-deductive paragraphs have a structural diagram similar to this one:

(1) Topic sentence—main idea
    (2) Direct support
        (3) Indirect support
    (4) Direct support
        (5) Indirect support
    (6) Direct support
        (7) Indirect support
(8) Conclusion

Complex-deductive paragraphs can have numerous variations. The number of direct supporting sentences can vary, as can the number of indirect supports. Sometimes direct supports may not require any indirect supports.

Consider another example of a complex-deductive paragraph:

(1) Two of the most popular inventory flow assumptions used by businesses today are FIFO (first-in, first-out) and LIFO (last-in, first-out). (2) FIFO assumes that the first goods purchased for inventory are the first goods sold. (3) Therefore, ending inventory under FIFO consists of the most recent purchases. (4) Because older, usually lower costs are matched with sales revenues, FIFO results in a higher net income and thus higher income tax liabilities. (5) The LIFO flow assumption, on the other hand, assumes that the most recent purchases are the first goods sold. (6) Ending inventory under LIFO will consist of older, usually less expensive goods. (7) Cost of goods sold, however, will be based on more recent, higher prices. (8) Thus LIFO usually results in lower net income and lower income tax liabilities. (9) This advantage makes LIFO very popular with many businesses.

This paragraph can be outlined to reveal the following structure:

I. Topic sentence (1): Two popular inventory flow assumptions
  A. FIFO (2–4)
    1. Description (2)
    2. Effect on inventory (3)
    3. Effect on net income and taxes (4)

B. LIFO (5–9)
   1. Description (5)
   2. Effect on inventory (6)
   3. Effect on net income and taxes (7–8)
   4. Popularity (9)

The descriptions of FIFO and LIFO in this paragraph are, of course, very condensed—probably too condensed for most purposes. Moreover, the paragraph is really too long. It would probably be better to divide it between sentences four and five. The result would be two shorter, but closely related paragraphs. Both would have simple-deductive structures. However, the first paragraph would be a modified version of a simple-deductive structure, because the main idea of this paragraph would be the second sentence.

The important idea about both simple- and complex-deductive paragraphs is their unity; all sentences, either directly or indirectly, develop the main idea of the paragraph as expressed in the topic sentence.

Some writers may wonder about a third type of paragraph organization— paragraphs with an inductive arrangement of ideas. Inductive paragraphs put the main idea last; supporting sentences lead up to the topic sentence, which is, of course, the last sentence in the paragraph.

For most business writing, inductive paragraphs are not as effective as simple- or complex-deductive paragraphs. Business readers like to identify main ideas from the start; they don't like to be kept in suspense, wondering "What's all this leading up to? What's the point?" So it is a good idea to stick with deductive organization for most, if not all, of your paragraphs.

Paragraph Development

An effective paragraph is not only well organized; it is also well developed. That is, the idea expressed in the topic sentence is adequately explained and illustrated so that the reader has a clear understanding of what the writer wishes to say.

Several techniques are useful for paragraph development: illustrations or examples, definitions, descriptive and factual details, and appeals to authority.

Probably the most useful technique of paragraph development is illustrations or examples—typical cases or specific instances of the idea being discussed. Illustrations can take a variety of forms. Sometimes a paragraph will combine several brief examples, or it may use one long, extended illustration. The examples may be factually true, or they may be hypothetical—invented for the purpose of illustration. A good writer will often combine illustrations with other techniques of paragraph development.

Definitions are particularly useful to explain concepts or terms which might be unfamiliar to the reader. A definition can be formal, such as the meaning given in a dictionary or an accounting standard, or it can be a more informal explanation of a term. Frequently a definition is more effective when combined with an illustration.

Here is a paragraph developed by definition and illustration:

> *Assets* can be defined as "economic resources—things of value—owned by a business."[1] For example, cash is an asset; so are the land, buildings, and equipment owned by a business. Sometimes assets are resources legally owned by a business, though not tangible. An example of this kind of asset is an account receivable.

Descriptive and factual details give a more thorough, concrete explanation of the idea expressed in a general way in the topic sentence. Factual details give measurable, observable, or historical information that can be objectively verified. Descriptive details are similar to factual details; they give specific characteristics of the subject being discussed.

The following paragraph combines definition, detail, and illustration:

> The matching principle relates revenues generated during a period with the expenses required to produce those revenues. Thus revenues earned from sales are matched with such expenses as production costs, advertising, and sales commissions. Accurately matching expenses with revenues results in a truer picture of a business's profitability during a given period of time.

Finally, some paragraphs are developed by appeals to authority—facts, illustrations, or ideas obtained from a reputable source such as a book, article, interview, or official pronouncement. Appeals to authority may be paraphrases—someone else's idea expressed in your own words—or direct quotations from the source being used. The paragraph at the top of this page uses a direct quotation from an accounting textbook to provide an authoritative definition of *assets*. Chapter 11 gives more information on the correct use of quotations and paraphrases.

By using a variety of techniques, then, effective writers fully develop the ideas expressed in the topic sentences of their paragraphs. Illustration, definition, factual and descriptive detail, and authority—all of these techniques give the reader a clear understanding of what the writer wishes to explain.

However you decide to develop your paragraphs, remember the importance of your reader's interests and needs. It is usually good to select supporting details and examples with which the reader is already familiar.

TRANSITIONS

Transitions, which are another essential element of coherent writing, link ideas together. They can be used between sentences, paragraphs, and major divisions of the writing. Their purpose is to show the relationship between two ideas: how the second idea flows logically from the first, and how both are related to the main idea of the entire document.

As an example of how transitions work, consider again this complex-deductive paragraph. The topic sentence (main idea) is the first sentence; the transitional expressions are in italics.

(1) Financial statements are important to a variety of users. (2) *First,* investors and potential investors use the statements to decide if a company is a good investment risk. (3) These users look at such factors as net income, the debt-to-equity ratio, and retained earnings. (4) *Second,* creditors use financial statements to decide if a firm is a good credit risk. (5) Creditors want to know if a firm has a large enough cash flow to pay its debts. (6) *Third,* governmental agencies analyze financial statements for a variety of purposes. (7) *For example,* the Internal Revenue Service will want to know if the company has paid the required amount of taxes on its income. (8) These examples of financial statement users show how diverse their interests can be.

The sentences beginning *first* (2), *second* (4), and *third* (6) give three examples of the paragraph's main idea: the variety of financial statement users. These three sentences relate to one another in a logical, sequential way, which the transitions make clear. These sentences also relate directly to the topic sentence; they illustrate it with specific examples. Sentence 7, which begins with *for example,* relates only indirectly to the main idea of the paragraph, but it relates directly to sentence 6. Sentence 7 expresses one example of the purposes financial statements have for government agencies.

Transitions can express a number of relationships between ideas. In the above paragraph, the transitions indicate an enumerated list (2, 4, and 6) and a specific illustration of a general statement (7). Transitions can also imply other relationships between ideas—conclusions, additional information, or contradiction, for example.

To illustrate further the importance of transitions within a paragraph, look at the following example, which lacks transitions:

Incorporation offers several advantages to businesses and their owners. Ownership is easy to transfer. The business is able to maintain a continuous existence even when the original owners are no longer involved. The stockholders of a corporation are not held responsible for the business's debts. If the XYZ Corporation defaults on a $1,000,000 loan, its investors will not be held responsible for paying that liability. Incorporation enables a business to obtain professional managers with centralized authority and responsibility. The business can be run more efficiently. Incorporation gives a business certain legal rights. It can enter into contracts, own property, and borrow money.

Now see how much easier it is to read the paragraph when it has appropriate transitions:

Incorporation offers several advantages to businesses and their owners. *For one thing,* ownership is easy to transfer, *and* the business is able to maintain a continuous existence even when the original owners are no longer involved. *In addition,* the stockholders of a corporation are not held responsible for the business's bad debts. *For example,* if the XYZ Corporation defaults on a $1,000,000 loan, its investors will not be held responsible for paying that liability. Incorporation *also* enables a business to obtain professional managers with centralized authority and responsibility; *therefore,* the business can be run more efficiently. *Finally,* incorporation gives a business certain legal rights. *For example,* it can enter into contracts, own property, and borrow money.

Transitional Words and Phrases

Following is a list of frequently used transitional expressions, their meanings, and example sentences showing how some of them work.

Adding a point or piece of information:
and, also, in addition, moreover, furthermore, first/second/third, finally
Accounting is a demanding profession. It can also be financially rewarding.

Making an exception or contrasting point:
but, however, nevertheless, on the other hand, yet, still, on the contrary, in spite of..., nonetheless
The use of historical cost accounting has many drawbacks. Nevertheless, it is still the basis of most accounting procedures.

Giving specific examples or illustrations:
for example, for instance, as an illustration, in particular, to illustrate
Financial statements serve a variety of users. For example, investors use them to evaluate potential investments. Other kinds of uses include...

Clarifying a point:
that is, in other words, in effect, put simply, stated briefly
The basic accounting equation is *assets equal liabilities plus owners' equity.* That is, $A = L + OE$.

Conceding a point to the opposite side:
granted that, it may be true that, even though, although
Although generally accepted accounting principles are not perfect, their use may offer considerable assurance that financial statements are presented fairly.

Indicating place, time, or importance:
Place: above, beside, beyond, to the right, below, around
Time: formerly, hitherto, earlier, in the past, before, at present, now, today, these days, tomorrow, in the future, next, later on, later
Importance: foremost, most importantly, especially, of less importance, of least importance
In earlier centuries there was no need for elaborate accounting systems. But the size and complexities of today's businesses make modern accounting a complicated process indeed.

Indicating the stages in an argument or process, or the items in a series:
initially, at the outset, to begin with, first, first of all, up to now, so far, second, thus far, next, after, finally, last of all
The accounting process works in stages. First, transactions must be analyzed.

Giving a result:
as a result, consequently, accordingly, as a consequence, therefore, thus, hence, then, for that reason
Generally accepted accounting principles allow flexibility in their application. Therefore, accountants are able to meet the changing needs of the business world.

Summing up or restating the central point:
in sum, to sum up, to summarize, in summary, to conclude, in brief, in short, as one can see, in conclusion
In conclusion, transitions often make writing much easier to read.

Repetition of Key Words and Phrases

Effective writers use transitional expressions not only between sentences, but also between paragraphs and between major divisions of the document. However, to create continuity between these larger units, they may also use an additional technique—repetition of key words or phrases. The typical location for these repetitions is at the beginning of a new paragraph or section. The following outline of a student's paper shows the structure of a discussion on alternatives to historical cost accounting. Notice how the combination of transitional expressions and repeated key phrases holds the parts of the report together. These techniques also tie the parts of the report to the main idea of the paper, which is summarized in the thesis statement. Notice also how summary sentences appear throughout the outline.

The Monetary Unit Assumption[2]

I. Introductory paragraph
   A. Attention-getting sentences
      One of the basic assumptions accountants made in the past was that money was an effective common denominator by which business enterprises could be measured and analyzed. Implicit in this assumption was the acceptance of the stable and unchanging nature of monetary units. Recently, however, the validity of this assumption has been questioned not only by academicians and theorists, but by practitioners as well.
   B. Thesis statement (main idea of entire paper)
      Several solutions have been proposed by accountants to correct for the changing value of the monetary unit.
II. Body
   A. Nature of the problem
      The unadjusted monetary unit system has been criticized because it distorts financial statements during periods of inflation.
   B. First solution to the problem
      1. One solution to overstating profits solely because of inflation is to adjust figures for changes in the general purchasing power of the monetary unit. (This paragraph describes this solution and its advantages.)
      2. However, the general purchasing power approach has been criticized for several reasons. (The paragraph describes the disadvantages of this approach.)
   C. Second solution to the problem
      1. Instead of the general purchasing power procedure, some favor adjusting for changes in replacement cost. (Paragraph describes this solution.)
      2. One of the major advantages of the replacement cost approach. . .(Paragraph discusses several advantages.)

3. One authority has summarized the criticisms of replacement cost accounting: "Most of the criticisms. . . ." (Paragraph discusses the disadvantages of this approach.)
III. Concluding paragraph
Adjusting for changes in the general purchasing power and adjusting for changes in replacement cost represent attempts to correct the problems of the stable monetary unit assumption in times of inflation.

Pronouns Used to Achieve Coherence

Another tool that effective writers use to achieve coherent writing is the pronoun. A pronoun stands for a noun or a noun phrase that has previously been identified. The noun that the pronoun refers to is called its *antecedent*. Consider the following sentence:

Firms usually issue their financial statements at least once a year.

In this sentence, the pronoun *their* refers to the noun *firms*. Put another way, *firms* is the antecedent of *their*.

Because pronouns refer to nouns that the writer has already used, pronouns help connect the thoughts of a paragraph. Look at how the pronouns work in this paragraph:

The audit staff reviewed the financial statements of Tristram Industries to determine if the statements had been prepared in accordance with generally accepted accounting principles. *We* found two problems that may require us to issue a qualified opinion. First, Tristram has not been consistent in *its* treatment of contingencies. Second, *we* identified several transactions that may violate the concept of substance over form. Thus, *we* suggest a meeting with Tristram's management to discuss these issues.

Pronouns require a word of warning, however. Unless a writer is careful, the reader may not be sure what noun the pronoun refers to. Look at the problem in this sentence:

The managers told the accountants that they did not understand company policy.

Who doesn't understand company policy—the managers or the accountants? This sentence illustrates the problem of ambiguous pronoun reference. Chapter 5 discusses this problem further.

Problems with Transitions

Two problems can occur with the use of transitions, other than the failure to use them when they are needed. The first problem occurs when a writer uses transitional expressions too often. These expressions are necessary to make the relationship of ideas clear when there might be some confusion. Frequently, however, this logical relationship is clear without the use of transitional expressions. Read this paragraph again:

> Accountants never finish their education. They work hard for their college degrees, but after college they must continue studying to stay current on the latest developments in the profession. They must be thoroughly familiar with changing governmental regulations and new pronouncements by professional organizations like the FASB. To improve their professional competence, they participate in a variety of continuing education programs sponsored by such organizations as the AICPA and state accounting societies. Indeed, well-qualified accountants will be lifetime students, always seeking better ways to serve their clients and the public.

Notice how easy this paragraph is to follow, even though it does not use a single transitional expression.

The second problem that can occur with transitions is to use the wrong expression, so that an illogical connection of ideas is suggested. Consider these examples:

FAULTY TRANSITION: GAAP are not established by federal law. For instance, organizations such as the FASB issue these standards, and the FASB is not part of the federal government.
REVISED: GAAP are not established by federal law. Rather, organizations that are not part of the federal government, such as the FASB, issue these standards.
FAULTY TRANSITION: If accountants do not follow GAAP, they may lose their CPA licenses. Therefore, they must follow GAAP to conform to their code of professional ethics.
REVISED: If accountants do not follow GAAP, they may lose their CPA licenses. They must also follow GAAP to conform to their code of professional ethics.

Writing with coherence, then, requires that you use a number of techniques so that your writing is easy to follow and main ideas stand out. Remember to use summary statements throughout the paper, short paragraphs with clear topic sentences, and transitions to tie your ideas together smoothly.

This chapter has added four rules to our list of effective writing skills. We now have seven rules:

1.   **Analyze the purpose of the writing and the needs of the readers.**
2.   **Use an outline to organize the ideas you want to present.**
3.   **Write the draft, and then revise it to make the writing polished and correct.**
4.   **Make the writing unified—all sentences should relate to the main idea, either directly or indirectly. Eliminate digressions and irrelevant detail.**
5.   **Use summary sentences and transitions to make your writing coherent.**
6.   **Write in short paragraphs that begin with clear topic sentences.**
7.   **Develop paragraphs by illustration, definition, detail, and appeals to authority.**

EXERCISES

Exercise 3-1

Peter Dowling is a junior staff accountant for a small CPA firm in Austin, Texas. The senior partners have asked him to investigate two computer systems for possible purchase by the firm. The partners have also asked him to recommend the system that the firm should buy. Peter has drafted the following outline for his report and asked for your critique.

    I. Introduction
   II. The history of computer technology
  III. Simple Sam Computer Model B-13
       A. General description of features
       B. Nearest service center in Dallas, Texas
       C. Can handle much of the firm's computer work
       D. Limited capacity for future expansion
       E. Takes up only a small amount of office space
   IV. Whiz Kid Computer Model 1004
       A. Easily adaptable in the future to new programs and functions
       B. Slightly larger than the Simple Sam Model
       C. Service center in Austin
       D. Can handle all the firm's current computer work
       E. General description of features
    V. The need for accountants to have more training in computer science
   VI. The role of computers in the future of accounting
  VII. Conclusion

1. What is the purpose of Peter's report?
2. What do you think is the main idea of the report?
3. What material included in Peter's outline is irrelevant to his purpose?
4. What necessary information has he forgotten to include?
5. Are the ideas in the outline arranged logically? If not, rearrange the ideas into a more effective outline. Include only relevant material.
6. What kinds of transitional devices could Peter use when he writes his report? Rewrite the outline in sentence form, and include transitional devices.

Exercise 3-2

Identify the transitional devices (transitional expressions, repetition of key words and phrases, pronouns) in the following paragraphs. Note how logically these devices tie the sentences together.

1. (1) Under the FIFO method, ending inventory will consist of the last units purchased. (2) Accountants often favor this method of accounting for inventories because it is easier to apply and more logical than some of the other methods. (3) FIFO also gives a more current inventory value on the balance sheet. (4) However, FIFO may result in a misleading earnings figure during times of inflation.
2. (1) The use of the specific identification method of inventory accounting is relatively time-consuming and costly. (2) Also, a business could use this method to manipulate

earnings by recording the lowest possible price for a particular item sold and thus increase earnings on that item. (3) Because of these problems, the specific identification method is not recommended for most businesses.

3. (1) The vast bulk of purchases (and sales) throughout the world are conducted on a *credit* basis rather than on a *cash* basis. (2) This "buy now, pay later" attitude is particularly prevalent in dealings among manufacturers, wholesalers, and retailers. (3) Indeed, the extension of credit seems to be a major lubricant of the world's economies. (4) Thus, unless a customer is considered a dangerous credit risk, cash is not expected until a later date. (5) Furthermore, an "authorized signature" of the buyer is usually sufficient; no formal promissory note is necessary. (6) This practice is known as buying (or selling) on open account; the debt is shown on the buyer's balance sheet as an account payable.[3]

Exercise 3–3

For the following paragraphs, identify

- Topic sentence
- Structure (simple-deductive, complex-deductive)
- Major and minor supporting ideas in complex-deductive paragraphs
- Transitional devices
- Techniques of development (single or multiple examples, definition, factual and/or descriptive detail, appeal to authority, or a combination of techniques)

1. (1) One career alternative for accounting graduates is to work for a government. (2) Government accountants oversee the financial records of federal, state, and local agencies. (3) They also examine the records of individuals and businesses that are subject to government regulations. (4) Employees of the Internal Revenue Service, for example, often examine business records supporting tax returns. (5) Performing services similar to management accountants, government accountants also budget administrative costs and plans for future operations, record transactions and events, and electronically process accounting data for government bureaucracies.[4]

2. (1) The accounting profession may be classified in many ways; a major classification is public accounting and private accounting. (2) "Public" accountants are those whose services are rendered to the general public on a fee basis. (3) Such services include auditing, income taxes, and management consulting. (4) "Private" accountants are all the rest. (5) They consist of not only those individuals who work for businesses but also those who work for government agencies, including the Internal Revenue Service.[5]

3. (1) An accounting system is a formal means of gathering data to aid and coordinate collective decisions in light of the overall goals or objectives of an organization. (2) The accounting system is the major quantitative information system in almost every organization. (3) An effective accounting system provides information for three broad purposes or ends: internal reporting to managers, for use in planning and controlling routine operations; internal reporting to managers, for use in strategic planning—that is, the making of special decisions and the formulating of overall policies and long-range plans; and external reporting to stockholders, government, and other outside parties.[6]

4. (1) Purchase options on land represent payments to the owners of property giving one the right during a specified period to buy a site or pass up the purchase oppor-

tunity. (2) Accounting for these options presents problems for today's accountant. (3) He or she must decide whether to capitalize the cost of the option in a land account or to expense the cost in the immediate period. (4) Further complications exist when clients acquire several options on suitable sites with intentions of choosing the best alternative. (5) Here, the accountant must consider several factors before recording the costs incurred, including materiality and future expectations.[7]

Exercise 3–4

Some of the following paragraphs are effetively organized, but some lack unity and/or coherence. Analyze the paragraphs to decide which ones need revision. Then revise the faulty paragraphs, using some of these techniques.

- a strong topic sentence stating the paragraph's main idea
- transitional devices showing the relation between sentences
- elimination of sentences that don't fit
- division of long, disunified paragraphs into shorter, unified ones
- rearranging sentences by grouping relevant ideas together (add sentences if necessary)

1. Government accountants help national, state, and local governments control spending and budgeting. Government spending could run rampant. Governmental accounting is similar to industrial accounting in many of its functions. Government accountants help prevent the government from wasting taxpayers' money.

2. One service that public accountants perform is auditing. Accountants examine clients' financial statements to see if they are in conformity with generally accepted accounting principles. Accountants give credibility to financial statements. Public accountants offer management consulting services. Management consultants suggest ways firms can improve such functions as information processing, budgeting, and accounting systems. Taxes are an increasingly complex area. Accountants prepare and file returns and advise clients how to incur the smallest tax liability on a transaction.

3. Many corporations can benefit from convertible debt. Firms should be aware of the hardships that may arise from conversion or nonconversion. Firms should be aware that accounting requirements impose a potentially unfavorable effect on earnings per share. Corporations want to obtain low-cost funds now, and desire also to increase their equity in the future.

4. Although the purchase of our supplier's stock may offer us several advantages, there are also some potential problems we should consider. For one thing, we may not always need the supplier's raw material, because we may not always manufacture the product that requires this material. And even if we continue to manufacture our product, our research and development staff may develop a cheaper, synthetic raw material. Finally, if we do purchase the stock but later need to resell it, we cannot be assured that the stock will be marketable at that time.

Exercise 3–5

Write a sentence outline for one of the following topics. Assume the outline is for a 500–1,000 word report that you are preparing for your client, Eleanor Johnson. Eleanor is the owner/manager of a small jewelry store with 10 employees. She is astute about business matters, but she has little training in accounting.

Include in your outline a sentence stating the main idea or purpose of the report. Divide your subject into logical subtopics, stating in a sentence the main idea of each division. Finally, show the transitional devices you would use to tie the report together. (For a model outline, see page 28 of this chapter.)

TOPICS:

1. How to reconcile a bank statement.
2. Internal control for cash in Eleanor Johnson's store. (You may want to narrow this topic to one aspect of internal control, such as control over the cash registers.)
3. Possible causes for low inventory turnover in the store's china department. (Invent some possible causes for this hypothetical situation.)

Exercise 3-6: Writing Topics

Discuss the following topics in well-organized and well-developed paragraphs. Remember the techniques for effective paragraphs: unity, coherence, length, structure, and development.

1. Conservatism
2. Foreign Corrupt Practices Act
3. Internal control
4. Reversing entries
5. Stockholders' equity
6. Cash
7. Responsibility accounting
8. Capitalization
9. Cost center
10. Direct labor
11. FASB
12. GAAP
13. Tax deferral
14. Double entry accounting

ANSWERS TO EXERCISES

Answers, Exercise 3-1

1. The purpose of Peter's report is to compare the two computer systems and to recommend the better system for his firm.
2. The report's main idea might be stated like this:
    Because of its several advantages—adaptability to future use, versatility for present use, convenient location of the service center—the Whiz Kid system would be the wiser purchase.

3. Outline sections II, V, and VI are irrelevant to the report's purpose. The history of computer technology, the need for accountants to have more computer training, and the role of computers in the future of accounting will not affect the choice of computer systems for Peter's firm.

4. Answers to this question will vary. Perhaps most obviously, Peter has forgotten to include the systems' costs in his outline.

5. Here is one possible outline for Peter's report:

   I. Introduction, including the main idea
  II. Whiz Kid Model 1004
      A. General description of features
      B. Costs
      C. Advantages
         1. Can handle all the firm's current computer work
         2. Easily adaptable for expansion in the future
         3. Service center is in Austin
      D. Disadvantage: slightly larger than the Simple Sam model
 III. Simple Sam Model B-13
      A. General description of features
      B. Costs
      C. Advantages
         1. Can handle all of the firm's current computer work
         2. Takes up only a small amount of office space
      D. Disadvantages
         1. Limited capacity for future expansion
         2. Nearest service center in Dallas, Texas

6. Peter could expand the outline to indicate transitional devices:

   I. Introduction
      Main idea: Because of its several advantages—adaptability to future use, versatility for present use, convenient location of service center—the Whiz Kid system would be the wiser purchase.
  II. The best computer system for our firm is probably the Whiz Kid Model 1004.
      A. This model has a number of features that make it suitable for a firm such as ours. For example,...
      B. The Whiz Kid computer is relatively inexpensive to purchase and operate.
      C. This computer will offer several important advantages for our firm. First,...
      D. Although the Whiz Kid offers all these attractive features, it does have one drawback.
 III. Another system that might be suitable for our firm is the Simple Sam Model B-13.
      A. This computer offers many of the same features as the Whiz Kid Model 1004.
      B. The Simple Sam computer is also comparable to the Whiz Kid computer in terms of cost.
      C. This computer does offer one important advantage to our company: it would take up only a small amount of office space.
      D. However, the Simple Sam System has two disadvantages that may limit it for our purposes. For one thing,...
  IV. Conclusion
      Thus, in spite of the additional office space it will require, I recommend the Whiz Kid because of its many advantages for our firm.

Answers, Exercise 3-2

1. (2) it—pronoun
       method/methods, inventories—
       repetition of key words
    (3) FIFO, inventory—repetition of key words
       also—transitional expression
    (4) FIFO—repetition of key word
       however—transitional expression
2. (2) method—repetition of key word
       also, thus—transitional expressions
    (3) specific identification method—repetition of key phrase
3. (3) credit—repetition of key word
    (4) credit, cash—repetition of key words
       thus—transitional expression
    (5) furthermore—transitional expression
    (6) buyer—repetition of key word

Answers, Exercise 3-3

1. • Topic sentence: (1)
    • Structure: complex-deductive
    • Supports:
      major: (2), (3), (5)
      minor: (4)
    • Transitional devices:
      (2) government—repetition of key word
      (3) they—pronoun
         also—transitional expression
         government—repetition of key word
      (4) for example—transitional expression
      (5) government accountants—repetition of key phrase
         also—transitional expression
         government—repetition of key word
    • Techniques of development:
      details, examples
2. • Topic sentence: (1)
    • Structure: complex-deductive
    • Supports:
      major: (2), (4)
      minor: (3), (5)
    • Transitional devices:
      (2) public—repetition of key word
      (3) services—repetition of key word
      (4) private, accountants—repetition of key words
      (5) they—pronoun
    • Techniques of development:
      details, examples
3. • Topic sentence: (1)
    • Structure: simple-deductive

- Transitional devices:
    - (2) accounting system, organization—repetition of key phrase and word
    - (3) accounting system, information, decisions—repetition of key phrase and words
      that is—transitional expression
- Techniques of development: definition, details

4.
- Structure and supporting sentences: The structure of this paragraph is not easy
  to analyze. The topic sentence is the second sentence; sentence (1) is a supporting
  sentence—a definition.

  We might decide that this paragraph is simple-deductive, although some people
  would argue that it is complex. As a complex-deductive paragraph, it would have
  the following structure:
    - (1) major support
    - (2) topic sentence
    - (3),(4) major supports
    - (5) minor support
- Transitional devices:
    - (2) options—repetition of key word
    - (3) he or she—pronouns
    - (4) options—repetition of key word
    - (5) here—transitional expression
- Techniques of development:
  definition, details

Answers, Exercise 3-4

1. This paragraph needs revision. Here is one possibility:

   Government accountants help national, state, and local governments control
   spending and budgeting. Without controls, government spending could run rampant.
   Thus, one function of government accountants is to help prevent the government
   from wasting taxpayers' money.

2. This paragraph also needs revision:

   Public accountants offer a variety of services to the public. One such service is
   auditing. An auditor examines a client's financial statements to see if they are fair
   and prepared in conformity with generally accepted accounting principles.
   Accountants thus give credibility to a firm's financial statements. Another service
   that the public accountant offers is management consulting services. Management
   consultants suggest ways firms can improve such functions as information
   processing, budgeting, and accounting systems. Finally, public accountants may
   aid the public in the increasingly complex area of taxes. Tax accountants prepare
   and file tax returns and advise clients how to incur the smallest tax liability on a
   transaction.

3. This paragraph also needs revision. One possibility:

   Many corporations can benefit from convertible debt, especially corporations that
   want to obtain low-cost funds now, and also desire to increase their equity in the
   future. However, firms considering convertible debt financing should be aware of
   the hardships that may arise from conversion or from nonconversion; they should
   also be aware that accounting requirements impose a potentially unfavorable effect
   on earnings per share.[8]

4. This paragraph is acceptable as it is written.

NOTES

1. Jack E. Kiger, Stephen E. Loeb, and Gordon S. May, *Accounting Principles,* 2nd ed. (New York: Random House, 1987), p. 1062.

2. Steven C. Dabbs, "The Monetary Unit Assumption" (unpublished student paper, University of Georgia, 1978).

3. Charles T. Horngren, *Introduction to Financial Accounting,* 3rd ed. (Englewood Cliffs, N.J.: Prentice-Hall, Inc., © 1987), p. 12. Reprinted by permission.

4. Allan Bashinski, "Accounting Careers" (unpublished student paper, University of Georgia, 1982).

5. Adapted from Horngren, *Introduction to Financial Accounting,* p. 5. Reprinted by permission.

6. Charles T. Horngren, *Introduction to Management Accounting,* 7th ed. (Englewood Cliffs, N.J.: Prentice-Hall, Inc., © 1987), p. 3. Reprinted by permission.

7. Greg Thompson, "Land Option Costs" (unpublished student paper, University of Georgia, 1982).

8. Jean Bryan, "Finance and Accounting Considerations in Issuing Convertible Debt" (unpublished student paper, University of Georgia, 1980).

CHAPTER 4
A Sense of Style: Writing with Conciseness and Clarity

So far in this book we have looked at writing mainly as an organizational task: planning the structure and contents of the paper so that it achieves its purpose in a way the readers will find meaningful. We have stressed the quality of coherence: writing that is easy to follow, with main ideas that stand out. Previous chapters have looked at writing in terms of large units. They have discussed the structure of the paper as a whole, and the organization of sections and paragraphs.

We turn now to a more detailed level of effective writing. This chapter looks at the choices of words and construction of sentences that contribute to a vigorous, readable writing style. In this discussion of style, we will emphasize two other important qualities of effective writing: conciseness and clarity.

CONCISENESS

Chapter 3 has already suggested several ways to make your writing more concise. The fourth rule of effective writing stresses the importance of eliminating digressions and irrelevant detail. In general, we can define concise writing as that which contains no unnecessary elements—no extra words, phrases, sentences, or paragraphs.

Be concise—make every word count.

Unnecessary Words

The easiest way to be concise (make every word count) is to see how many words you can cross out of your writing, often with only a simple revision of the sentence. Beware of dead words—words that fill up space without adding meaning. Here are some examples of sentences littered (and padded) with dead words:

WORDY:	There are several advantages to historical cost accounting. (8 words)
CONCISE:	Historical cost accounting offers several advantages. (6 words)
WORDY:	There is one organization that has been very influential in improving the profession of accounting—the AICPA. (17 words)
CONCISE:	The AICPA has influenced the accounting profession positively. (8 words)
WORDY:	We hope the entire staff will assist us in our efforts to reduce costs. (14 words)
CONCISE:	We hope the entire staff will help us reduce costs. (10 words)
WORDY:	The estimates range all the way from $100 to $350. (10 words)
CONCISE:	The estimates range from $100 to $350. (7 words)

Watch out for "there is" and "there are." They can usually be eliminated. "The fact that," "which is," and "which are" can sometimes be left out:

WORDY:	I would like to call your attention to the fact that our earnings last month were down fifty percent. (19 words)
CONCISE:	Remember that our profits were down fifty percent last month. (10 words)
	or (even better)
	Our profits dropped fifty percent last month. (7 words)
WORDY:	In spite of the fact that our costs rose by ten percent, we still were able to keep our prices stable. (21 words)
CONCISE:	Although costs rose by ten percent, our prices remained stable. (10 words)
WORDY:	His partner, who is an engineer,...
CONCISE:	His partner, an engineer,...

Simplicity

Another way to make your writing concise is to write as simply as possible. Sometimes writers get into the habit of using big words and long, complicated sentences. Such writing is hard to read. Look at the following sentence:

An increase in an employee's rate of pay will not become effective prior to the date on which the employee has completed a minimum of 13 weeks' actual work at his regular occupational classification.

If we simplify this sentence, its meaning will be easier to understand:

An employee must work at least 13 weeks at his regular job before he can receive an increase in pay.[1]

Sometimes words and sentences get so complicated that their meaning is completely lost:

Ultimate consumer means a person or group of persons, generally constituting a domestic household, who purchase eggs generally at the individual stores of retailers or purchase and receive deliveries of eggs at the place of abode of the individual or domestic household from producers or retail route sellers and who use such eggs for their consumption as food.

Translation:

Ultimate consumers are people who buy eggs to eat them.[2]

Therefore, another technique for effective writing style is simplicity.

Keep it simple—simple vocabulary and short sentences.

Good writers will use short, everyday words as much as possible. For example, they will write *use* instead of *utilize, help* instead of *assistance.* Shorter, familiar words are easier to read and make writing more forceful.

The chart on pages 41–44 shows two columns of words. Column B lists short, familiar words; Column A lists longer, more difficult words that are often substituted for the everyday words in Column B. The chart also shows how single words ("because") can often replace phrases ("for the reason that"). As a general rule, use the words and phrases in Column B rather than those in Column A. Some of the terms in Column A can be omitted entirely ("it should be noted that").

Another way to achieve a simple, readable style is to use short sentences. *The average sentence should be about 15 to 20 words long.* Short sentences are particularly important when you are explaining complicated ideas.

Note that 15 to 20 words is an *average.* Some sentences will be longer, some shorter. In fact, it is a good idea to vary sentence lengths so the writing does not become monotonous. Sentence variation will be discussed again later in this chapter (see pages 53–54).

SIMPLIFYING WORD CHOICES

As a rule, use the words and phrases in Column B rather than those in Column A.

COLUMN A	COLUMN B
above-mentioned firms	these firms
absolutely essential	essential
activate	begin
advise	tell
aggregate	total
anticipate	expect
along the lines of	like
assist	help
as per your request	as you requested
at all times	always
at this point in time	now
at this time	now
attempt	try
communicate	write, tell

commence	begin
completely eliminated	eliminated
comprise	include
consider	think
constitute	are, is
disutility	uselessness
demonstrate	show
discontinue	stop
due to the fact that	because, since
during the time that	while
earliest convenience	promptly
effort	work
enclosed herewith	enclosed
enclosed please find	enclosed is
endeavor	try
exercise care	be careful
facilitate	ease, simplify
failed to	didn't
few in number	few
for the purpose of	for
for the reason that	since
from the point of view that	for
furnish	send, give
i.e.	that is
implement	carry out
in advance of	before
in many cases	often
in all cases	always
in most cases	usually
inasmuch as	since
in behalf of	for
in connection with	about
indicate	show, point out
initiate	begin
in terms of	in
in the amount of	of, for
in the case of	if
in the event that (of)	if
in the nature of	like
in the neighborhood of	about
in this case	here
investigate	study
in view of the fact that	because, since
it has come to my attention	Ms. Jones has just told me; I have just learned

it is felt	I feel; we feel
it is our understanding that	we understand that
it should be noted that	omit
maintain	keep
maintain cost control	control cost
make application to	apply
make contact with	see, meet
make a purchase	buy
maximum	most, largest
minimum	least, smallest
modification	change
obtain	get
on the order of	about
on the part of	by
optimum	best
past history	history
per annum	annually, per year
period of time	time, period
pertaining to	about, for
philosophy	plan, idea
please be advised that	omit
please don't hesitate to call on us	please write us
prepare an analysis	analyze
presently	now
prior to	before
procure	get, buy
provide continuous indication	indicate continuously
provide	give
pursuant to your inquiry	as you requested
range all the way from	range from
regarding	about
relative to	about
represent	be, is, are
require	need
so as to	to
subsequent to	after, later
substantial	large, big
sufficient	enough
terminate	end, stop
the major part of	most of
the manner in which	how
the undersigned; the writer	I, me
through the use of	by, with
true facts	facts
thereon, thereof, thereto, therefrom	omit

this is to acknowledge	thank you for, I have received
this is to inform you that we shall send	we'll send
transpire	happen
under separate cover	by June 1, tomorrow, separately, by parcel post
until such time as	until
utilize	use
vital	important
with a view to	to
with reference to	about
with regard to	about
with respect to	on, for, of, about
with the object to	to
with the result that	so that

Verbs and Nouns

Another technique to make writing more concise is to use active verbs and descriptive nouns, rather than lots of adverbs and adjectives.

Write with active verbs and descriptive nouns.

See how this sentence can be improved:

WORDY: There are some serious, unfortunate results of accounting based on historical cost during times of decreasing purchasing power of the monetary unit. (22 words)

CONCISE: Historical cost accounting creates problems during periods of inflation. (9 words)

One frequent cause of wordy writing is hidden verbs. For example,

causes a misstatement of
instead of
misstates

provides a matching of
instead of
matches

makes an analysis of
instead of
analyzes

will serve as an explanation of
instead of
will explain

What are the hidden verbs in these sentences?

We should not make reference to any prior years' financial statements in our report.

The company's history of marginal performance over the past several years may be an indication of future solvency problems.

In the first sentence, the hidden verb is *refer;* in the second sentence it is *indicate.* The revised sentences are a little less wordy, a little more forceful:

We should not refer to any prior years' financial statements in our report.

The company's history of marginal performance over the past several years may indicate future solvency problems.

Here are some other sentences with hidden verbs, followed by revisions to make them more concise:

HIDDEN VERB: This method will result in a distribution of the costs between the balance sheet and the income statement.
REVISED: This method will distribute the costs between the balance sheet and the income statement.
HIDDEN VERB: We are able to make the determination of the historical cost of an asset due to the fact that we have records of its purchase.
REVISED: We can determine an asset's historical cost because we have records of its purchase.
HIDDEN VERB: One can propose an argument that we should recognize the entire amount.
REVISED: One can argue that we should recognize the entire amount.

Finally, avoid sentence introductions that weaken the sentence idea. Don't apologize or over-qualify what you say:

WORDY: This report is an attempt to explain the proper accounting treatment for loss contingencies. (14 words)
CONCISE: This report explains accounting for loss contingencies. (7 words)
WORDY: This is to acknowledge receipt of your letter of June 1. (11 words)
CONCISE: Thank you for your letter of June 1. (8 words)
WORDY: This is to inform you that we are sending a check in the amount of $798.14. (16 words)
CONCISE: We're sending a check for $798.14. (6 words)

In summary, clear, readable writing contains no unnecessary or dead words. Be concise—your writing will gain in forcefulness.

CLARITY

When your writing is concise it will also be clear, because important ideas will not be buried in unnecessary words and details. Writing as simply as possible will also help you achieve clarity, since you will be using words the reader knows and feels comfortable with.

Other techniques for improving the clarity of your writing include the careful use of jargon and precise, concrete word choices.

Jargon

Jargon is "The specialized or technical language of a . . . profession."[3] We all know what accounting jargon is. It is words and phrases like *amortization, accrual, debit, GAAP,* and *deferred income taxes.*

One kind of jargon is acronyms: words composed of the first letter of a group of words, such as FASB, GAAP, and LIFO. The general rule for acronyms is to write out the words of the acronym the first time you use it, with the acronym in parentheses.

> One of the earliest groups to set accounting standards was the Committee on Accounting Procedure (CAP).

After you have identified the acronym fully, you can use the acronym alone throughout the rest of the document.

Unless you use jargon, including acronyms, carefully, it will detract from the clarity of your writing.

Two guidelines can help you decide when to use jargon, and when to look for other words. The first is to remember the needs of your readers, and to use language that they will understand. A fellow accountant will probably understand what you mean by straight-line depreciation, but managers or clients who have not studied accounting may be unfamiliar with the term. But be careful when using jargon even with your accounting colleagues. Would everyone with a degree in accounting know what you mean by an operating lease?

The second guideline for the use of jargon is to remember always to keep your word choices as simple as possible. Avoid jargon when ordinary language will say what you mean. For example, why say "the bottom line" if you mean net income or loss?

Of course, jargon is often unavoidable when you need to communicate technical information as efficiently as possible. But once again, remember the needs of your readers: define or explain technical terminology with which they may not be familiar.

Use jargon only when your readers understand it. Define technical terms when necessary.

Precise Meaning

One of the most important elements of clear writing is precision. That is, meanings are clear and yield only one possible interpretation. Precision is particularly important in accountants' writing, because accountants are often legally responsible for the accuracy of what they write. Moreover, the technical nature of accounting makes precise writing a necessity. One rule for an effective writing style is, thus, precision.

Be precise—avoid ambiguous and confused meanings.

Imprecise writing can result from several causes. One culprit is poor diction, or the inaccurate use of words:

> The major *setback* of the current method is verifiability.
> (Poor diction. The writer meant *drawback*.)

> The advantage of measurements in terms of replacement costs is that the costs reflect *what the item is worth.*
> (What is the precise meaning of the italicized phrase? *Worth* is vague.)

In these examples the diction problems are italicized:

POOR DICTION:	The reason for this purchase was to *help from* liquidating LIFO layers.
REVISED:	The reason for this purchase was to prevent the liquidation of LIFO layers.
POOR DICTION:	This memo will discuss how to account for the *theft* of the filling station.
	(This sentence says that the filling station itself was carried off.)
REVISED:	This memo will discuss how to account for the robbery at the filling station.

Unclear, awkward writing can also result from the misuse of words ending in *-ing*:

UNCLEAR:	The lease does not meet the 90 percent test, therefore classifying the lease as an operating lease.
REVISED:	The lease does not meet the 90 percent test, so it must be classified as an operating lease.
AWKWARD AND UNCLEAR:	By forming larger inventory groups the chances of liquidating an early LIFO layer are reduced.
REVISED:	Larger inventory groups reduce the chances of liquidating an early LIFO layer.
	(Note: This revision also changes the sentence from passive to active voice—see pages 51–53).

Another cause of imprecise writing is misplaced and dangling modifiers. With a misplaced modifier, the modifying word or phrase is not placed next to the sentence element it modifies, which leads to a confusing, and sometimes humorous, result.

> Periodic inventory systems are often used by businesses that sell a large volume of inexpensive items *like grocery stores and drugstores.*
> (The italicized phrase appears to modify *items*, but it really modifies *businesses*.)

Periodic inventory systems are often used by businesses, such as grocery stores and drugstores, which sell a large volume of inexpensive items.

Consider another sentence with a misplaced modifier:

This technique identifies tax returns for audits with a high probability of error.

Revised:

This technique identifies, for audit, tax returns with a high probability of error.

Dangling modifiers, which usually come at the beginning of a sentence, do not actually modify any word in the sentence. Usually the word modified is implied, rather than stated directly. Look at this sentence:

After buying the bonds, the market price will fluctuate.

The writer probably meant something like this:

After we buy the bonds, the market price will fluctuate.

Faulty pronoun reference can also cause writing to be ambiguous and confusing:

Capitalization of interest is adding interest to the cost of an asset under construction which increases its book value.

The meaning of this sentence is unclear. What increases book value? The pronoun *which* is confusing; its reference is vague. Here is one possible revision:

Capitalization of interest is adding interest to the cost of an asset under construction. The result is an increase in the asset's book value.

Faulty pronoun reference can be labelled vague, ambiguous, or broad. These terms all mean that the writer doesn't make clear what the pronoun refers to. The pronoun *this* is particularly troublesome.

FAULTY REFERENCE:	The use of generally accepted accounting principles does not always produce the true financial position of a company. This is a problem for the FASB.
REVISED:	The use of generally accepted accounting principles does not always produce the true financial position of a company. This weakness in the principles is a problem for the FASB.

A good rule is never to use *this* by itself. Add a noun or phrase to define what *this* is.

Another pronoun that can cause problems with reference is *it*:

FAULTY REFERENCE: The inventory valuation can follow the physical flow of goods, but it is not necessary.

REVISED: The inventory valuation can follow the physical flow of goods, but this correspondence is not necessary.

Misplaced and dangling modifiers and faulty pronoun reference are grammatical problems, and will be discussed further in Chapter 5. However, writing can be grammatically correct and still be imprecise. Consider again this sentence:

The major drawback of the current value method is verifiability.

Revised:

The major drawback of the current value method is *the lack of* verifiability.

The revision makes quite a difference in meaning!

Often, the ability to write precisely is a function of precise reading—and thinking. An accounting professor assigned his Accounting 801 students two papers for the quarter. He then wrote the following statement on the board:

Accounting 801 students who complete the course will write a total of two papers this quarter. True or false?

The precise thinkers in the class realized that the statement might not be true. The students could write papers for other classes as well. Thus, some students could write *more than* a total of two papers for the quarter.

Learn to analyze carefully what you read. Then you will be able to perfect your own writing so that your meanings are clear and precise.

Here are some other examples of sentences revised to improve their clarity:

UNCLEAR: This bond is not considered risky because it sells at only 70 percent of its maturity.

REVISED: The selling price of this bond, which is 70 percent of its maturity value, does not necessarily indicate that the bond is risky.

UNCLEAR: When purchasing bonds at a discount, the investment cost is less than the face value of the investment.

REVISED: When bonds sell at a discount, the investment cost is less than the face value of the investment.

UNCLEAR: When reviewing the prior auditor's workpapers, no recognition of a possible obsolescence problem was found.

REVISED: When reviewing the prior auditor's workpapers, we found no recognition of a possible obsolescence problem.

UNCLEAR: Historical cost accounting has several problems which do not consider inflation and changing prices.

REVISED: Historical cost accounting causes several problems because it does not take into account inflation and changing prices.

Concrete Wording

Chapter 3 discussed the use of concrete facts, details, and examples as a way to develop paragraphs. Writing that is concrete adds clarity to your writing and makes it much more interesting to your readers.

Concrete writing can be explained by defining its opposite, abstract writing. Abstract writing is vague, general, or theoretical. It is hard to understand because it is not illustrated by particular, material objects. Concrete writing, on the other hand, is vivid and specific; it brings a picture into the mind of the reader.

Illustrations of abstract and concrete writing styles will make them easier to understand.

ABSTRACT

Historical cost is important in accounting. It is easy for accountants to use, and it is often seen in the financial statements. Historical cost has some disadvantages, but it has its good points, too.

CONCRETE

Historical cost often refers to the amount of money actually paid for an object at the time it was purchased. For example, if a truck was purchased in 1987 for $10,000, then $10,000 would be the truck's historical cost. Many accountants favor historical cost accounting because the values of assets are easy to determine from invoices and other records of the original purchase. However, in times of inflation the historical cost of an asset may not indicate its true value. For example, an acre of land bought in 1950 for $5,000 might be worth several times that amount today, but it would still be recorded in the owner's books, and the statement of financial position, at its historical cost. Thus one disadvantage of historical cost accounting is that it often undervalues assets.

By giving more detailed information and specific, concrete examples of historical cost, the second paragraph makes this concept easier to understand and more interesting to read.

In the following examples, vague, abstract sentences are replaced by more concrete writing:

VAGUE: Accountants should write well.
REVISED: Accountants need to write clear, concise letters to their clients and other business associates. (This sentence replaces the vague *well* by indicating two characteristics of effective writing: clarity and conciseness. The revision also gives an example of one type of accountants' writing—letters to clients and associates.)
VAGUE: The financial statements are interesting.
REVISED: Smith Corporation's earnings statement for 1989 shows a net loss of $5,437,000.

OR

Smith Corporation's financial statements for 1989 contain information that stockholders may find alarming. For example, the earnings statement shows a net loss of $5,437,000.

Be concrete—use facts, details, and examples.

READABLE WRITING

If your writing is interesting to read, it will almost always be clear. Lively, natural sentences hold your readers' attention and keep them involved in what you are saying, so they have an easier time understanding your ideas.

The remainder of this chapter will be devoted to several techniques that will make your sentences readable and clear: the use of active voice, writing with variety and rhythm, and questions of tone.

Passive and Active Voice

This technique for achieving a good writing style may seem technical, but it too will become clear after a few definitions and examples.

Use active voice for most sentences.

First of all, we should define active and passive voice. Sentences are usually written in active voice. The subject of the sentence performs the action described by the verb.

ACTIVE: Most corporations issue financial statements at least once a year.

Passive voice, on the other hand, describes action done *to* somebody or something *by* another agent; the agent is not always named in the sentence.

PASSIVE: Financial statements are issued (by most corporations) at least once a year.

This formula will help you identify most passive voice verbs:

Passive Voice = a form of the + the past participle of another verb
verb *to be*   (usually ending in *-ed*)

FORMS OF THE VERB *TO BE:*	TYPICAL PAST PARTICIPLES:
is, are, were, was, been, being, be, am	accrued, received, used, computed, given, kept

Sometimes passive verb phrases also contain a form of *to have* (has, have, had, etc.) or an auxiliary (will, should, would, must, etc.), but passive voice always contains a *to be* form plus a past participle.

Active-voice sentences are often clearer than passive-voice sentences. Consider these examples:

PASSIVE: Taxes *were increased* by 50 percent.
               (In this example, most readers would want to know *who* raised taxes.)
ACTIVE: Congress *increased* taxes by 50 percent.
PASSIVE: Deliberate understatement of assets and stockholders' equity with the intention of misleading interested parties *is prohibited.*
ACTIVE: SEC regulations *prohibit* deliberate misstatement of assets and stockholders' equity if the intention is to mislead interested parties.

Unfortunately, writers of "officialese," especially in government, business, and research, have so badly overused passive voice that we tend to accept it as standard style. But passive voice is seldom effective—it lacks the forcefulness and clarity of active voice. Compare the following pairs of sentences:

PASSIVE: If reversing entries are used the possibility of bookkeeping errors is reduced.
ACTIVE: Using reversing entries reduces the possibility of bookkeeping errors.
PASSIVE: In many college accounting courses effective writing skills are emphasized.
ACTIVE: Many college accounting courses emphasize effective writing skills.
PASSIVE: When we purchased the building, it should have been recorded as an asset.
ACTIVE: When we purchased the building, we should have recorded it as an asset.
PASSIVE: In SAS No. 1 it is required that items such as these be disclosed in the financial statements.
ACTIVE: SAS No. 1 requires that the financial statements disclose items such as these.
PASSIVE: The second general standard of field work requires that independence, in both fact and appearance, be maintained by the auditor.
ACTIVE: The second general standard of field work requires that the auditor maintain independence in both fact and appearance.

Good writers will avoid using passive voice in most situations. They will ask themselves two questions. What is the action (verb)? Who or what is doing it (subject)?

Occasionally, of course, you will need to use passive voice to avoid awkward writing. For example, passive voice may be necessary to avoid an awkward repetition of sentence subjects. But use active voice whenever you can.

One word of warning: avoid substituting a weak active verb for passive voice. Be particularly careful of colorless verbs like *to exist* and *to occur.* The following sentences are written in active voice, but the sentences are weak:

Capitalization of option costs on land subsequently purchased should occur.

FIFO bases itself on the assumption that the first inventory acquired is the first inventory sold.

Try to find descriptive, vigorous verbs to substitute for weak verbs, or reword the sentence.

We must capitalize option costs on land subsequently purchased.

The assumption that underlies FIFO is that the first inventory acquired is the first inventory sold.

If you cannot think of a strong active verb, or if the sentence is awkward in active voice, then leave it in passive.

> Option costs on land subsequently purchased should be capitalized.
>
> FIFO is based on the assumption that the first inventory acquired is the first inventory sold.

A final consideration about active and passive voice is that sometimes you may want to emphasize the passive subject. For example, you would say

> The company was robbed.

rather than

> Some person or persons unknown robbed the company.

Variety and Rhythm

Another way to make your writing natural and more readable is to add variety.

Vary vocabulary, sentence lengths, and sentence structures. Read the writing aloud to hear how it sounds.

The purpose of sentence variety is to avoid monotony—a sing-song, awkward repetition of the same sentence rhythms, or overuse of a word or phrase. Read the following paragraph aloud.

> Financial analysts use ratios to analyze financial statements. Ratios show a company's liquidity. The current ratio shows the ratio of current assets to current liabilities. Ratios also show a company's solvency. The equity ratio is an example of a solvency ratio. It shows the ratio of owners' equity to total assets. Ratios also show profitability. The return-on-investment ratio is an example. It shows the ratio of net earnings to owners' equity.

This paragraph does not sound pleasing. In fact, it could easily lull the reader to sleep. The sentences are too similar in length and structure, and the word *ratio* is repeated too often. Let us try again.

> Ratios based on financial statements can reveal valuable information about a company to investors, creditors, and other interested parties. Liquidity ratios show whether a company can pay its debts. The quick ratio, for example, is a good indication of debt-paying ability for companies with slow inventory turnover. Ratios can also indicate a company's solvency; the equity ratio, for instance, shows the percentage of owners' equity to total assets. Investors in bonds use this figure to evaluate the safety of a potential investment. Finally, ratios can give a measure of

a company's profitability, which is of special interest to potential investors. The earnings-per-share ratio is probably the most popular of the profitability ratios.

Another cause of monotonous sentences is too many prepositional phrases, particularly when they are linked together to form a chain. Look again at the sentence below. Prepositions are circled; the rest of the phrase is underlined.

There are some serious, unfortunate results of accounting based on historical cost during times of decreasing purchasing power of the monetary unit.

This sentence contains a chain of prepositional phrases five links (phrases) long. A good rule is to avoid more than two prepositional phrases in a row.

If you are not sure what prepositions are, here is a partial list:

across, after, as, at, because of, before, between, by, for, from, in, in front of, in regard to, like, near, of, on, over, through, to, together with, under, until, up, with

Variety is an important element of readable writing because it gives sentences and paragraphs a pleasing rhythm. Read your paragraphs aloud. If you notice a word or phrase repeated too often, look for a synonym. If the sentences sound choppy and monotonous, vary their structures and lengths. Often a change in the way sentences begin will improve the rhythm of the paragraph. Add an occasional short sentence, and an occasional longer one (but be sure longer sentences are still easy to understand). And be careful of too many prepositional phrases. You do not want to bore your reader, and varied sentences are one way to keep your writing lively.

Tone

The tone of a document is the way it makes the reader feel, or the impression it makes. A letter can have a formal or informal tone, be personal or impersonal. It can be apologetic, cold, humorous, threatening, arrogant, respectful, or friendly.

Chapter 3 mentioned the need to vary your tone according to who the reader will be. If you are writing to a colleague who is also a good friend, you can be much more informal than if you are writing to someone you know only in a business relationship. Be particularly careful to show respect to those who are much older than you or in higher positions of authority.

One way to decide on the proper tone of a document you are writing is to put yourself in the position of your readers, and to write from their point of view. This approach is called writing with the "you attitude."

First of all, the "you attitude" requires that you be courteous. Treat your correspondent with tact, politeness, and respect. Avoid abruptness, condescension, and stuffiness—or any other form of rudeness. Here are some examples of poor tone:

This is a complicated subject, so I have tried to simplify it for you. (This sentence is condescending; it implies that the reader may not be very bright.)

I acknowledge receipt of your letter and beg to thank you. (Too formal and artificial—stuffy, in fact.)

Send me that report immediately. I can't understand why it has taken you so long to prepare it. (In certain situations you might *think* this way, but you'll get better results if you write with tact and courtesy.)

The use of personal pronouns (you, I, we) can contribute to the "you attitude." Keep the first person singular pronouns (I, me, my) to a minimum; focus instead on the reader with second person (you, your) or, in some cases, first person plural (we, us, our).

A personal tone, including personal pronouns, is especially effective when the message you are conveying is good news or neutral information. However, when you must write bad news or some sort of criticism, it is better to be impersonal and passive in order to be tactful:

TACTLESS: You failed to submit the form to the IRS on time.
  BETTER: The form wasn't submitted to the IRS on time.
      OR: The IRS didn't receive the form on time.

Another guideline for an effective tone is to stress the positive: what can be done rather than what cannot:

NEGATIVE: Because you were late in sending us your tax information, we cannot complete your tax return by April 15.
POSITIVE: Now that we have the information on your taxes, we can complete your tax return. We will request an extension of the deadline so that you will not be fined for a late filing.

Finally, be honest and sincere; avoid exaggeration and flattery.

In the final analysis, the guidelines for an effective writing tone are the same as those for good relationships. Learn to view a situation from the other person's point of view, and communicate in a way that shows your empathy and respect.

Here, then, is the final guideline for an effective writing style.

Write from the reader's point of view. Use tone to show courtesy and respect.

This chapter on style has added nine rules to our list of effective writing techniques. We now have 16 rules.

1. **Analyze the purpose of the writing and the needs of the readers.**
2. **Use an outline to organize the ideas you want to present.**

3. Write the draft, and then revise it to make the writing polished and correct.
4. Make the writing unified—all sentences should relate to the main idea, either directly or indirectly. Eliminate digressions and irrelevant detail.
5. Use summary sentences and transitions to make your writing coherent.
6. Write in short paragraphs that begin with clear topic sentences.
7. Develop paragraphs by illustration, definition, detail, and appeals to authority.
8. Be concise—make every word count.
9. Keep it simple—simple vocabulary and short sentences.
10. Enliven sentences with active verbs and descriptive nouns.
11. Use jargon only when your readers understand it. Define technical terms when necessary.
12. Be precise—avoid ambiguous and confused meanings.
13. Be concrete—use facts, details, and examples.
14. Use active voice for most sentences.
15. Vary vocabulary, sentence lengths, and sentence structures. Read the writing aloud to hear how it sounds.
16. Write from the reader's point of view. Use tone to show courtesy and respect.

EXERCISES

Exercise 4–1

Revise the following sentences so that they are written as simply and concisely as possible. Be alert for hidden verbs.

1. To determine how to account for our lease, we will make reference to *Statement of Financial Accounting Standards No. 13.*
2. The history of Elliot Industry's performance, which is marginal at best, may be an indication of solvency problems that will occur in the future.
3. A number of problems have come to light that may make it necessary for us to issue an opinion that is other than unqualified.
4. I have attempted to explain the three proposed alternatives for recording the cost of the land that has been purchased.
5. It is my recommendation that New York Corporation choose to value the asset at $95,000.
6. As you are no doubt aware, in the economic environment of today, having these services available from a firm with experience is indispensable and quite valuable.
7. I am in need of improved writing skills.
8. In conclusion, I would like to state that I feel this seminar is an excellent opportunity.
9. There are several benefits that can come from attending the seminar.
10. I hope this memo will exhibit the reasons why the conference will be beneficial.
11. The benefits of this educational program will avail themselves to the corporation via language and letters which are fresh, accurate, and clear.
12. Per the discussion held with you during our recent visit, there are several control objectives within the above-mentioned cycles that need to have techniques established or refined to ensure that these objectives are met.

13. These techniques will provide for an increased understanding of the problem.
14. Enclosed please find the information you will need to make an analysis of our inventory control.
15. We hope to begin production of our new product line before the end of this year.
16. Utilization of linear models alone may lead to unnecessary limitations as to the inferences that one may be able to draw from the data.
17. When executing the purchase of land, there are a number of costs incurred.
18. This method provides proper matching of expenses to revenues.

Exercise 4–2

Review the lists of simplified word choices on pp. 41–44 of this chapter. Then, without looking at the lists again, write a shorter and/or simpler version of the following words and phrases.

EXAMPLE:

	Simplify to:
in all cases	always

1. i.e.
2. enclosed please find
3. facilitate
4. initiate
5. prior to
6. so as to
7. the major part of
8. make a purchase
9. make an analysis
10. for the purpose of
11. in the amount of
12. optimum
13. maintain cost control
14. the writer
15. this is to acknowledge
16. under separate cover
17. with reference to
18. utilize
19. transpire
20. investigate
21. in the nature of
22. please be advised that
23. terminate
24. pursuant to your inquiry
25. failed to
26. at this point in time

27.   in advance of
28.   due to the fact that
29.   exercise care
30.   pertaining to
31.   it should be noted that

Exercise 4-3

Identify the jargon in the following sentences.

1.   GAAP require us to issue financials annually.
2.   The FASB will issue an exposure draft on that topic next month.
3.   We can issue convertible debt to improve our equity position.
4.   Negative cash flows may affect our position with our creditors.
5.   Credit Cash for $200.
6.   The historical cost of the machinery will be easy to determine.
7.   Our client must file a Schedule A with his return.
8.   Because of his income this year, he will be able to recapture.
9.   We must issue a qualified opinion on this audit.
10. According to SFAS 13, this lease qualifies as an operating lease.

Exercise 4-4

The meaning of the following sentences is not clear. Revise the sentences so that they are unambiguous and precise.

1.   After reading the following discussion, a recommendation will present the best method for our company.
2.   Each alternative has its rational for use.
3.   The FASB has not officially written a pronouncement on the handling of acquisition costs.
4.   Proponents claimed that the proposed legislation would provide changes from the old method of depreciation that would increase deductions and simplify computations.
5.   The report was concerned with the Accelerated Cost Recovery System as modified by the Tax Act of 1986. Its purpose was . . . .
6.   All companies incur expenses that do not provide future benefits to keep their business going to produce revenue.
7.   Capitalization states that once a cost expires, we should capitalize expense.
8.   Calculating the present value of the bonds' principal and future cash flows will determine our risk.
9.   The riskiness of these bonds does not depend on their selling price.
10. Under LIFO the lower costs are assigned to inventory which causes the cost of inventory to increase.

Exercise 4–5

The following sentences are abstract or vague. Revise them, using facts, details, or examples to make them more concrete. You may need to replace one vague sentence with several concrete sentences, or even a short paragraph. Alternatively, you could introduce a short paragraph with an abstraction and then develop the idea with more concrete, specific sentences. Feel free to invent details that will make the ideas more specific.

1. Internal control is important.
2. Sometimes firms keep two sets of records.
3. We must record this asset at its true value. (Hint: what is "true value"?)
4. The audit did not satisfy me.
5. The firm sold the asset for its cost. (Hint: what cost?)
6. Accounting for leases is tricky.
7. The nature of this asset requires us to capitalize it.
8. The accountant in charge of accounts receivable is not doing his job.
9. These stocks look like a good buy.
10. Accountants must use good judgment.

Exercise 4–6

Identify the passive-voice construction in the following sentences and revise them to active voice. Be careful not to substitute weak active verbs for passive voice. For some sentences you may need to invent a subject for the active verb.

EXAMPLE:

PASSIVE: That alternative could have been followed.
ACTIVE: We (or the firm, our client, McDonough Corporation, etc.) could have followed that alternative.

1. I have explained the three proposed alternatives for recording the cost of the equipment that has been purchased.
2. The option kept the land available until a decision was reached.
3. The accounts receivable aging is distorted by the journal entries.
4. Inventory should be controlled by the general ledger.
5. These disclosures are required for external reporting.
6. This procedure can easily be implemented.
7. It is recommended that finished parts inventories be physically controlled.
8. Most journal entries are reviewed by accounting management.
9. The opinion to be issued on the 1989 financial statements must be qualified.
10. Although our computer was purchased last year, it is already obsolete.
11. Each month our company's net income is reduced by accrued expenses.
12. At the seminar guidelines will be provided for lease accounting.

Exercise 4–7

Identify the prepositional phrases in the following sentences. Where too many phrases are linked together, revise the sentence.

EXAMPLE:

The problem of Breland Company is solved through the selection of one of the accounting methods presented.
Prepositional phrases identified:

The problem of Breland Company is solved through the selection of one of the accounting methods presented.

REVISED:

One of the accounting methods should solve Breland Company's problem.

1. Now that the choice of sites has been made and the expiration of options is occurring, this transaction must be recorded in the books of our firm correctly.
2. We have designed an audit program for use in future audits of the accounts receivable of ABC Company.
3. An accrual of expenses reports a more accurate picture of the operations of the current business period of the company.
4. The important issue to address in this company's situation is that of the expression of an opinion of the going concern.
5. The main problem of the staff is the determination of the cost at which to record the purchase.
6. The effect on our audit report of the sale of the bonds is twofold.
7. The return on an investment in bonds is based on the number of years to maturity and the current rate of interest in the market.
8. The calculation of the present values of the principal of the bonds and their cash flows will reveal our risk.
9. The amortization of the discount of the bond will allow us to realize the cash flows of the bond at an even rate throughout the life of the bond.
10. The determination of the net income of the company will pose no problem for the accountants in our department.

Exercise 4–8

Read the following paragraphs aloud; note their monotonous rhythms. Then revise the paragraphs so that they show greater variety in sentence structures and lengths. Note also when words or phrases are repeated too often.

1. Charter Air runs scheduled flights between several local communities. Charter Air also provides charter service for several local businesses. Charter's financial statements reveal marginal profits for the past several years. Last year Charter was forced to raise prices to compensate for increased fuel prices. These price increases and several economic downturns caused passenger volume to decline drastically.

Thus 1989 was a disastrous year for Charter Air. The preliminary information showed that 1989 losses were in excess of $2,000,000. This will force Charter Air into a deficit position. The 1988 balance sheet showed a net worth of $2,000,000 with total assets of $10,000,000.[4]

2. Every business sells products that may be returned. The customers may be unhappy with the product for many reasons. The customer may not like the size, style, or color. The customer may also simply change his or her mind. The supplier (vendor) calls these sales returns. The customer calls them purchase returns. Such merchandise returns are minor for manufacturers and wholesalers. They are major for retail department stores. Marshall Field's or Macy's may have returns of 12 percent of gross sales.[5]

Exercise 4–9

Revise the following paragraphs, using the techniques covered in this chapter as necessary.

1. If excess cash on hand is kept by a business, a loss for the business will result. Excess cash on hand brings in no benefits, while interest payments could be earned by the business. Investing cash on hand in government bonds would be a good thing for the company to do because it would be beneficial.

2. The purpose of this memo is an attempt to explain the three alternatives that have been proposed for recording the cost of the land that has been purchased by our company. The reasons for the recommendation I decided upon are discussed below along with the strong and weak points of the other proposed alternatives that I do not recommend. If one of these alternatives had been more consistent with GAAP, that alternative could have been followed. I hope you will be able to understand this discussion.

3. In order to find a suitable site for our new plant, we purchased three options on three pieces of land. The costs of all three options are thought to be necessary to find a site that will be suitable for our new plant. Since it is not impossible that all the three option costs will contribute to the economic benefit and to the general well-being of our company in the future, the amount that should be capitalized by our company includes the costs of all three of the options. Even though the company will choose only one site for purchase and eventually build the plant on it, the amount we should capitalize includes the costs of all three options. The reasoning is that the company uses all the options to decide on the site for the new plant.

4. Per the discussion that was held with you by our audit staff during their recent communication with you at your Denver office, there are several objectives for control within several accounting cycles that need to have control techniques and procedures established or refined to ensure that these objectives are met by your company. It is vital that all the objectives of control within each of these cycles have control objectives established or improved to provide assurance that the objective is achieved by the company in order to provide data that is accurate and timely, to preserve the integrity of the financial records of the company, and to maintain an adequate system of internal control, especially over the company's accounts receivable. In addition to the specific control techniques discussed in the following report, written procedures should be established so that data will be recorded in the way that management of the company intends.

ANSWERS

Answers, Exercise 4–1

1. To determine how to account for our lease, we will refer to *Statement of Financial Accounting Standards No. 13.*
2. Elliot Industry's history of marginal performance may indicate future solvency problems.
3. We have found several problems that may require us to issue a qualified opinion.
4. I have explained the three proposals for recording the cost of the purchased land.
5. I recommend that New York Corporation value the asset at $95,000.
6. In today's economic environment, having these services available from an experienced firm is invaluable.
7. I need improved writing skills.
8. In conclusion, this seminar is an excellent opportunity.
9. The seminar will benefit participants in several ways.
10. This memo will show why the conference will be beneficial.
11. The corporation will benefit if I attend the seminar because I will learn to make my memos and letters fresh, accurate, and clear.
12. During our recent visit we discussed the need for improved techniques to meet the control objectives within these cycles.
13. These techniques will help us understand the problem.
14. Enclosed is the information you will need to analyze our inventory control.
15. We hope to begin producing our new product line before the end of this year.
16. Use of linear models alone may limit unnecessarily the inferences we can draw from the data.
17. When a company buys land, it incurs a number of costs.
18. This method properly matches expenses with revenues.

Answers, Exercise 4–2

1. that is
2. enclosed is
3. ease, simplify
4. begin
5. before
6. to
7. most of
8. buy
9. analyze
10. for
11. of, for
12. best
13. control cost
14. I, me

15. thank you for
16. by June 1, separately, tomorrow, by parcel post
17. about
18. use
19. happen
20. study
21. like
22. omit
23. end, stop
24. as you requested
25. didn't, did not
26. now
27. before
28. because, since
29. be careful
30. about, for
31. omit

Answers, Exercise 4–3

1. GAAP, financials
2. FASB, exposure draft
3. convertible debt, equity position
4. negative cash flows
5. Credit, Cash. (Note: These terms have general meanings, but in this sentence they have technical accounting meanings that might not be familiar to a nonaccountant.)
6. historical cost
7. Schedule A, return
8. recapture
9. qualified opinion, audit
10. SFAS 13, operating lease

Answers, Exercise 4–4

1. The following discussion will conclude with a recommendation of the best method to use.
2. Each alternative has its rationale for use.
3. The FASB has not written an official pronouncement on the handling of acquisition costs.
4. Proponents claimed that the proposed legislation would provide changes from the old method of depreciation; these changes would increase deductions and simplify computations.
5. The report was concerned with the Accelerated Cost Recovery System as modified by the Tax Act of 1986. The purpose of the report was . . . .

6. All companies incur expenses that do not provide future benefits, yet these expenses keep the business going by producing revenue.
7. The rule for capitalization states that once a cost expires, we should capitalize the expense.
8. Calculating the present value of the bonds' principal and future cash flows will reveal our risk.
9. The selling price of these bonds does not indicate their riskiness.
10. Because LIFO assigns lower costs to inventory, the cost of goods sold increases.

Answers, Exercise 4–5

Answers will vary.

Answers, Exercise 4–6

Answers will vary, but here are some possibilities:

1. I have explained the three proposed alternatives for recording the cost of the equipment that our client has purchased.
2. The option kept the land available until we reached a decision.
3. The journal entries distort the accounts receivable aging.
4. The bookkeepers should use the general ledger to control inventories.
5. The SEC requires these disclosures for external reporting.
6. Management can easily implement this procedure.
7. The auditors recommend that we physically control finished parts inventories.
8. Accounting management reviews most journal entries.
9. We must qualify our opinion on the 1989 financial statements.
10. Although we purchased our computer last year, it is already obsolete.
11. Each month accrued expenses reduce our company's net income.
12. The seminar will provide guidelines for lease accounting.

Answers, Exercise 4–7

1. Now that the choice of sites has been made and the expiration of options is occurring, this transaction must be recorded in the books of our firm correctly.
   Now that we have chosen the site and the options have expired, we must record the transaction correctly in our books.
2. We have designed an audit program for use in future audits of the accounts receivable of ABC Company.
   We have designed a program for future audits of ABC Company's accounts receivable.
3. An accrual of expenses reports a more accurate picture of the operations of the current business period of the company.
   Accrued expenses report a more accurate picture of the company's current operations.
4. The important issue to address in this company's situation is that of the expression of an opinion of the going concern.
   Before we can issue our opinion, we must decide if this company is indeed a going concern.

Note: to address is an infinitive (a verb), not a prepositional phrase. However, too many infinitive phrases can also make a sentence awkward.

5. The main problem of the staff is the determination of the cost at which to record the purchase.
The staff's main problem is determining the cost at which to record the purchase.

6. The effect on our audit report of the sale of the bonds is twofold.
The bonds' sale has two effects on our audit report.

7. The return on an investment in bonds is based on the number of years to maturity and the current rate of interest in the market.
The bond's return on investment is based on the number of years to maturity and the market rate of interest.

8. The calculation of the present value of the principal of the bonds and their future cash flows will reveal our risk.
Calculating the present value of the bonds' principal and future cash flows will reveal our risk.

9. The amortization of the discount of the bond will allow us to realize the cash flows of the bond at an even rate throughout the life of the bond.
Amortizing the bond discount will allow us to realize the bond's cash flows evenly throughout the bond's life.

10. The determination of the net income of the company will pose no problems for the accountants in our department.
Determining the company's net income will pose no problems for our department's accountants.

Answers, Exercise 4–8

1. Charter Air runs scheduled flights between several of the local communities in the area and provides charter service for several local businesses. According to its previous financial statements, Charter Air has been marginally profitable in the past several years. During the past year, Charter Air was forced to raise its prices to compensate for increased fuel costs. Because of these price increases and the effects of the general economic downturns, passenger volume declined drastically, making 1989 a disastrous year for the company. The preliminary information showed that 1989 losses were in excess of $2,000,000. This loss will force Charter Air into a deficit position, as the 1988 balance showed a net worth of $2,000,000 with total assets of $10,000,000.

2. Every business sells products that may be returned. The customer may be unhappy with the product for many reasons, including color, size, style, quality, and a simple change of mind. The supplier (vendor) calls these sales returns; the customer calls them purchase returns. Such merchandise returns are minor for manufacturers and wholesalers but are major for retail department stores. For instance, returns of 12% of gross sales are not abnormal for stores like Marshall Field's or Macy's.

Answers, Exercise 4–9

The answers to this exercise will vary. The following lists identify the major weaknesses in each paragraph.

1. Passive voice, repetition of phrases, vague sentences, poor tone, wordy.
2. Wordy, passive voice, poor tone.
3. Repetitive, passive voice, wordy, too many prepositional phrases, sentences too long.

4. Wordy, passive voice, repetitive, sentences too long, verbs need simplifying, poor tone.

NOTES

1. George deMare, *How to Write and Speak Effectively* (New York: Price Waterhouse, 1958), p. 9.
2. Ibid., p. 11.
3. William Morris, ed., *The American Heritgage Dictionary of the English Language,* New College Edition (Boston: Houghton Mifflin Company, 1979), p. 701.
4. The revised paragraph (see p. 65 of the Answers) is from Doug Hertha, "Audit Report of Charter Air" (unpublished student paper, University of Georgia, 1982).
5. The revised paragraph (see p. 65 of the Answers) is from Charles T. Horngren, *Introduction to Financial Accounting,* 3rd ed. (Englewood Cliffs, N.J.: Prentice-Hall, Inc., © 1987), p. 214. Reprinted by permission.

CHAPTER 5
Grammar, Punctuation, and Spelling

Grammar, punctuation, and spelling are the technical details of good writing. Sometimes the rules may seem trivial or illogical, but they will help you achieve clarity and precision.

Accountants should have no trouble with precise detail. Think about how important the tiny decimal point is in a number! Punctuation marks can be just as important. Lawyers tell stories about misplaced commas in contracts costing clients thousands of dollars. Even though good punctuation, spelling, and grammar are seldom so dramatically important, they do contribute to polished, professional writing.

A mastery of English grammar tells the reader much about you as a person and as a professional. Your use of correct grammar says that you are an educated person who understands and appreciates the proper use of our shared language.

A grammatically correct document, free of mechanical and typographical errors, also shows that you know the importance of detail and are willing to spend the time necessary to prepare an accurate, precise document.

This chapter presents some of the most commonly made errors in grammar, punctuation, and spelling. Of course, only a few principles can be covered in this short space, so you should consult a basic English handbook for a complete list of rules and explanations. The discussion here focuses on rules that give accountants the most trouble.

MAJOR SENTENCE ERRORS

Major sentence errors include three kinds of problems: fragments, comma splices, and fused sentences. These errors have in common a serious flaw in the structure of the sentence.

Fragments

A sentence fragment is just what its name suggests: part of a sentence. You may recall that every sentence needs two essential elements, a subject and a verb. Often with sentence fragments, one of these elements is left out. Here are some examples:

> To account for the transaction correctly.
> (This phrase lacks a verb.)

> For example, *Statement of Accounting Concepts No. 13.*
> (This group of words also lacks a verb.)

> The reason being that we must cut costs in the shipping department.
> (*Being* is a present participle;* it cannot be substituted for a complete verb like *is* or *was.*)

> Although, our new computer system makes billing much faster.
> (This dependent clause has a subject and verb, but it cannot stand alone as a sentence because it is introduced by a subordinate conjunction,* *although.*)

Comma Splices

The second major sentence error is comma splices, which occur when independent clauses are combined by a comma alone.

An independent clause is a group of words with a subject and a verb; it can stand alone as a sentence. Here are two independent clauses punctuated as separate sentences:

> Increases in assets are recorded as debits on the left side of a T-account. Decreases are recorded as credits on the right side.

Sometimes writers want to combine two independent clauses into one sentence. This can be done correctly in several ways.

1. Put a semicolon (;) between the clauses.
    Increases in assets are recorded as debits on the left side of a T-account; decreases are recorded as credits on the right side.
2. Combine the clauses with a comma and a coordinating conjunction (*and, but, for, or, nor, yet, so*).
    Increases in assets are recorded as debits on the left side of a T-account, and decreases are recorded as credits on the right side.
3. Combine the clauses with a semicolon, a conjunctive adverb, and a comma. (Conjunction adverbs include *however, therefore, that, consequently, that is, for example,*

*Consult a grammar handbook for explanations of technical grammatical terms such as these.

nevertheless, also, furthermore, indeed, instead, still.)
Increases in assets are recorded as debits on the left side of a T-account; however, the decreases are recorded as credits on the right side.

Study the following comma splices. The independent clauses are joined by a comma alone.

COMMA SPLICE: Accountants must not only understand accounting procedures, they must also be able to communicate effectively.

REVISED: Accountants must not only understand accounting procedures; they must also be able to communicate effectively.
Accountants must understand accounting procedures and be able to communicate effectively.

COMMA SPLICE: LIFO may result in a lower net income, therefore, a company has lower income tax liabilities.

REVISED: LIFO may result in lower net income; therefore, a company has lower income tax liabilities.

COMMA SPLICE: Accountants write many letters as part of their professional responsibilities, for example, they may write letters to the IRS.

REVISED: Accountants write many letters as part of their professional responsibilities. For example, they may write letters to the IRS.

COMMA SPLICE: These transactions were not recorded correctly, that is, they were not recorded in the proper accounts.

REVISED: These transactions were not recorded correctly; that is, they were not recorded in the proper accounts.

Fused Sentences

Fused sentences, which are also called run-on sentences, occur when two independent clauses are joined without any punctuation at all.

FUSED SENTENCE: Generally accepted accounting principles are not laws passed by Congress however, the code of professional ethics requires accountants to follow GAAP.

REVISED: Generally accepted accounting principles are not laws passed by Congress. However, the code of professional ethics requires accountants to follow GAAP.

FUSED SENTENCE: This equipment is not a long-term asset it can be expensed rather than capitalized.

REVISED: This equipment is not a long-term asset; it can be expensed rather than capitalized.

PROBLEMS WITH VERBS

The correct use of verbs is a complicated matter in any language, as you will appreciate if you have ever studied a foreign language. Fortunately, because English is the native language for most of us, we usually use verbs correctly without having to think about them. We just know what sounds right.

A few problems do tend to occur even in the writing of educated people. We will now look briefly at a few of those problems.

Tense and Mood

The *tense* of a verb depends on when the action described by the verb takes place.

PAST TENSE:	We *signed* the contract.
PRESENT TENSE:	We *are signing* the contract.
	OR
	Do we sign the contract now?
	OR
	Everyone *signs* the contract.
FUTURE TENSE:	We *will sign* the contract next week.

Usually the choice of tense is logical and gives writers few problems.

The *mood* of a verb, however, is a little more confusing than its tense. Three moods are possible: indicative (states a fact or asks a question), imperative (a command or request), and subjunctive (a condition contrary to fact). The subjunctive mood causes the most trouble, although we often use it without realizing it:

If I *were* you, I would attend the seminar.
(condition contrary to fact)

The most common use of the subjunctive is to follow certain verbs such as *recommend, suggest,* and *require:*

I recommend that the company depreciate the asset over five years.

I suggest that he meet with the sales representative next week to discuss the problem.

The SEC requires that we disclose that item on our financial statements.

One problem to avoid is an unnecessary shift in tense or mood:

TENSE SHIFT:	Before we *issued* an unqualified opinion, we *made* sure that the company *is* a going concern. (Shift from past tense to present.)
REVISED:	Before we issued an unqualified opinion, we made sure that the company was a going concern.
TENSE SHIFT:	Sales *dropped* by 20 percent last year. That drop *is* the result of increased competition. (Shift from past to present tense.)
REVISED:	Sales dropped by 20 percent last year. That drop was the result of increased competition.
MOOD SHIFT:	We *must credit* Cash to account for this transaction. Then *debit* Office Supplies. (Shift from indicative to imperative mood.)
REVISED:	We must credit Cash to account for this transaction and then debit Office Supplies.
MOOD SHIFT:	If we *increase* inventory, we *would service* orders more quickly. (Shift from indicative to subjunctive.)

REVISED: If we increase inventory, we will service orders more quickly.

OR

If we increased inventory, we would service orders more quickly.

MOOD SHIFT: If we changed our policy, we *will attract* more customers. (Shift from subjunctive to indicative.)

REVISED: If we changed our policy, we would attract more customers.

OR

If we change our policy, we will attract more customers.

Subject-Verb Agreement

Another major problem with verbs is subject-verb agreement. A verb should agree with its subject in number. That is, singular subjects take singular verbs; plural subjects take plural verbs. Note that singular verbs in the present tense usually end in *s*:

That (one) <u>man works</u> hard.

Those (two) <u>men work</u> hard.

Some irregular verbs (*to be, to have,* etc.) look different, but you will probably recognize singular and plural forms.

That <u>stock is</u> a good investment.

These <u>stocks are</u> risky.

The <u>ABC Corporation has</u> fifty accountants on its staff.

Some <u>corporations have</u> net earnings of more than a million dollars.

There are a few difficulties with this rule. First, some singular subjects are often thought of as plural. *Each, every, either, neither, one, everybody,* and *anyone* take singular verbs.

<u>Each</u> of the divisions <u>is</u> responsible for maintaining accounting records.

Second, sometimes phrases coming between the subject and the verb make agreement tricky.

The <u>procedure</u> used today by most large companies in their foreign divisions <u>is explained</u> in this article.

Finally, two or more subjects joined by *and* take a plural verb. When subjects are joined by *or,* the verb agrees with the subject closest to it.

Either <u>Company A or Company B is planning</u> to issue new stocks.

Either the <u>president</u> or the <u>managers have called</u> this meeting.

PROBLEMS WITH PRONOUNS

Pronouns cause two main problems, agreement and reference. Agreement is easy: a pronoun should agree with its antecedent (the word it stands for). Thus singular antecedents take singular pronouns, and plural antecedents take plural pronouns.

> Mr. Jones took his check to the bank.
>
> Each department keeps its own records.

This rule usually gives trouble only with particular words. Note that *company, corporation, firm, management,* and *board* are singular; therefore, they take singular pronouns.

> The company increased its profits by fifty percent. (Not *company—their.*)
>
> The Accounting Principles Board discussed accounting for intangible assets in its Opinion No. 17. (Not *Board—their.*)
>
> Management issued its report. (But: The managers issued their report.)

The second problem with pronouns is vague, ambiguous, or broad reference. This problem was discussed in Chapter 4, but here are some additional examples:

FAULTY REFERENCE:	Although our trucks were purchased last year, this year's revenue depends on them. *This* associates the true cost with this year's revenues.
REVISED (one possibility):	Although our trucks were purchased last year, this year's revenue depends on them. To associate the true cost with this year's revenue, we must apply the matching principle.
FAULTY REFERENCE:	Adjusting entries are needed to show that an expense has been incurred, but that it has not been paid. *This* is a very important step.
REVISED:	Adjusting entries are needed to show that an expense has been incurred, but that it has not been paid. Making these adjusting entries is a very important step.

While agreement and reference cause writers the most problems with pronouns, occasionally other questions arise.

One of these questions is the use of first and second person, which some people have been taught to avoid. In the discussion of tone in Chapter 4 we saw how the use of these personal pronouns can contribute to an effective writing style for many documents. Personal pronouns are not usually appropriate, however, in formal documents such as some reports and contracts.

There are a few other cautions about the use of personal pronouns. First, use first person singular pronouns (*I, me, my, mine*) sparingly to avoid writing that sounds self-centered. The second problem to avoid is using *you* in a broad sense to mean people in general, or as a substitute for another pronoun.

INCORRECT:	I don't want to file my income tax return late because the IRS will fine you.
REVISED:	I don't want to file my income tax return late because the IRS will fine me.

PROBLEMS WITH MODIFIERS

Chapter 4 discussed the two main problems that can occur with modifiers: (1) misplaced modifiers, which occur when the modifer is not placed next to the word it describes, and (2) dangling modifiers, which do not modify any word in the sentence.

MISPLACED MODIFIER:	We only sold five service contracts last year. (*Only* is misplaced. It should be next to the word or phrase it modifies.)
REVISED:	We sold only five service contracts last year.
DANGLING MODIFIER:	When preparing financial statements, GAAP must be adhered to.
REVISED:	When preparing financial statements, we must adhere to GAAP.

The best guideline for using modifiers correctly is to place them next to the word or phrase they describe.

PARALLEL STRUCTURE

Parallel sentence elements are those that are grammatically equal: nouns, phrases, clauses, etc. When these items appear in a list or a compound structure, they should be balanced. Nouns should not be matched with clauses, for example, nor sentences matched with phrases.

STRUCTURE NOT PARALLEL:	This report will discuss the system's purpose, how much it costs, and its disadvantages. (This sentence combines a noun, a dependent clause, and another noun.)
REVISED:	This report will discuss the system's purpose, cost, and disadvantages.
STRUCTURE NOT PARALLEL:	We recommend the following procedures:

- Hire a consultant to help us determine our needs. (phrase)
- Investigate alternative makes and models of equipment. (phrase)
- We should then set up a pilot program to test the new system. (sentence)

REVISED: We recommend the following procedures:
- Hire a consultant to help us determine our needs. (phrase)
- Investigate alternative makes and models of equipment. (phrase)
- Set up a pilot program to test the new system. (phrase)

APOSTROPHES AND PLURALS

The rules for apostrophes and plurals are quite simple, but many people get them confused.

Most plurals are formed by adding either *s* or *es* to the end of the word. If you are unsure of a plural spelling, consult a dictionary.

With one exception, apostrophes are never used to form plurals. Apostrophes are used to show possession. For singular words the form is *'s*. For plural words the apostrophe comes after the *s*.

SINGULAR	PLURAL
firm's capital	officers' salaries
statement's figures	users' interests
business's profits	businesses' profits

A commonly made mistake is *stockholders' equity*. When *stockholder(s)* is plural (it usually is), the apostrophe comes after the *s*.

There is one exception to the plural-apostrophe rule. Abbreviations, numerals, and letters can form their plurals with *'s:*

1980's or 1980s

CPA's or CPAs

Often a phrase requiring an apostrophe can be rewritten using *of* or its equivalent.

the company's statements (the statements of the company)

the month's income (the income of the month)

a week's work (the work of a week)

the year's total (the total for the year)

And note these possessive plurals:

two companies' statements

five months' income

three weeks' work

ten years' total

prior years' statements

"Ten years' total" might also be written "ten-year total." But analyze the difference in meaning between "ten-year total" and "ten years' totals."

Finally, some writers confuse *it's* with *its*. *It's* is a contraction of *it is; its* is the possessive pronoun.

It's important to make careful journal entries.

The company issued its statements.

COMMAS

The many rules for comma usage are sometimes hard to understand. However, commas are important because they often make sentences easier to understand. For example, the meaning of this sentence is ambiguous:

I would not worry because you appear to have a thriving business.

Adding a comma will clear up the confusion:

I would not worry, because you appear to have a thriving business.

Comma Guidesheet

USE COMMAS:

1. before *and, but, or, nor, for, so,* and *yet*—when these words come between independent clauses.
   The FASB issued a Discussion Memorandum, and many accountants responded with their opinions.

   Competition increased, but we still increased our earnings.

2. following an introductory adverbial clause.
   When investors read a company's financial statements, they are especially interested in the net income figure.

   Because production costs are up, we will be forced to raise our price.

   Although we worked all night, the report was still late.

   If we increase our inventory, we will need a new warehouse.

3. following transitional expressions and long introductory phrases.
   In the Statement of Financial Accounting Standards No. 2 (SFAS No. 2), the FASB defined its position on research and development costs.

To improve our sales in the southeast region, we are adding three new sales representatives. However, we still need four more representatives.

4.   to separate items in a series (including coordinate adjectives).
Accounting students must be intelligent, dedicated, and conscientious.

Send this report to the vice president, the manager of the shipping department, and the senior bookkeeper.

5.   to set off nonrestrictive clauses and phrases (compare rule 4, below).
The SEC, which is an agency of the federal government, is concerned with proper presentation of financial statements.

The annual report, which was issued in June, contained good news for investors.

The main office, located in Boston, employs 350 people.

6.   to set off contrasted elements.
Treasury stock is a capital account, not an asset.

We want to lower our prices, not raise them.

7.   to set off parenthetical elements.
Changes in accounting methods, however, must be disclosed in the financial statements.

"Our goal," he said, "is to dominate the market."

DO NOT USE COMMAS:

1.   to separate the subject from the verb or the verb from its complement.
Incorrect:
The company that manufacturers trucks, has an impressive net income.
Correct:
The company that manufactures trucks has an impressive net income.
2.   to separate compound verbs or objects.
Incorrect:
She wrote angry letters to the FASB, and the SEC.
Correct:
She wrote angry letters to the FASB and the SEC.
3.   to set off words and short phrases that are not parenthetical.
Incorrect:
Financial transactions are recorded, in journals, in chronological order.
Correct:
Financial transactions are recorded in journals in chronological order.
4.   to set off restrictive clauses, phrases, or appositives (compare rule 5, above).
Incorrect:
A problem, that concerns many accountants, is the use of historical cost in times of inflation.

Correct:
A problem that concerns many accountants is the use of historical cost in times of inflation.

5.   before the first item or after the last item of a series (including coordinate adjectives).
Incorrect:
Some asset accounts are noncurrent, such as, land, buildings, and equipment. (The faulty comma is the one before *land*.)
Correct:
Some asset accounts are noncurrent, such as land, buildings, and equipment.

COLONS AND SEMICOLONS

The rules of colons (:) are few and easy to master, although sometimes writers use them incorrectly. Used correctly—and sparingly—colons can be effective because they draw the readers' attention to the material that follows.

Colons can be used in the following situations:

1.   to introduce a series.
Three new CPA firms have located in this area recently: Smith and Harrison, CPAs; Thomas R. Becker and Associates; and Johnson & Baker, CPAs.

2.   to introduce a direct quotation, especially a long quotation that is set off from the main body of the text (see the following section).
The senior partner issued the following instruction: "All audit workpapers should include concise, well-organized memos summarizing any problem revealed by the audit."

3.   to emphasize a summary or explanation.
My investigation of Ace Manufacturing's financial situation led me to an important conclusion: Unless Ace attracts new capital immediately, it may be forced into bankruptcy.

4.   following the salutation in a business letter.
Dear Mr. Evans:

When a colon introduces a series, an explanation, or a summary, the clause that precedes the colon should be a complete statement.

We have increased our sales to the following customers: Elliot Industries, Anderson, Inc., and Trueblood Manufacturing.

Not

Our best customers are: Elliot Industries, Anderson, Inc., and Trueblood Manufacturing.

Semicolons (;) are used for only two situations: between independent clauses (see page 68) and between items in a series, if the items themselves have internal commas:

The proposal was signed by John Underwood, President; Alice Barret, Vice-President; and Sue Barnes, Treasurer.

DIRECT QUOTATIONS

The punctuation of direct quotations depends on their length. Short quotations (less than five typed lines) are usually run-in with the text and enclosed with quotation marks. Longer quotations are set off from the text—indented and single spaced—with no quotation marks. Direct quotations should be formally introduced; a colon may separate the introduction from the quoted material. Study the following examples:

> SFAS No. 14 defines an industry segment as a "component of an enterprise engaged in providing a product or service or a group of related products or services primarily to unaffiliated customers...for a profit."[1]

> SFAS No. 14 gives the following definition of an industry segment:

> > Industry segment. A component of an enterprise engaged in providing a product or service or a group of related products and services primarily to unaffiliated customers (i.e., customers outside the enterprise) for a profit. By defining an industry segment in terms of products and services that are sold primarily to unaffiliated customers, this Statement does not require the disaggregation of the vertically integrated operations of an enterprise.[2]

A direct quotation requires a citation identifying its source (see Chapter 11). In addition, it is better to identify briefly the source of a quotation within the text itself, as the above examples illustrate. If a quotation comes from an individual, use his or her complete name the first time you quote from this source.

> According to Richard Smith, an executive officer of the Fairways Corporation, "The industry faces an exciting challenge in meeting foreign competition."

Notice the placement of punctuation in relation to quotation marks:
Inside quotation marks:

| period | quotation." |
| comma | quotation," |

Outside quotation marks:

| colon | quotation": |
| semicolon | quotation"; |

Inside or outside quotation marks:

question mark ?" or "?
—depending on whether the question mark is part of the original quotation:

Mr. Misel asked, "Where is the file of our new client?"

Did Mr. Misel say, "I have lost the file of our new client"?

One final remark. Sometimes writers depend too heavily on direct quotation. It is usually better to paraphrase—to express someone else's ideas in your own words—unless precise quotation would be an advantage. As a rule, no more than 10 percent of a paper should be direct quotation. To be most effective, quotations should be used sparingly, and then only for authoritative support or dramatic effect.

SPELLING

Finished, revised writing should be entirely free of misspelled words. Keep a dictionary on your desk, and use it if you have any doubt about a word's spelling. Or, if you are using a word processor, use a spelling check program to eliminate misspelled words.

Spelling: If in Doubt, Look It Up!

The following short list contains words commonly misspelled by accountants:

accrual, accrued
advise/advice
affect/effect
cost/costs, consist/consists, risk/risks
led, misled
occurred, occurring, occurrence
principal/principle
receivable, receive
separate, separately

The italicized words in the following sentences are frequently confused.

Please *advise* us of your decision. (*Advise* is a verb.)

We appreciate your *advice*. (*Advice* is a noun.)

This change in accounting policy will not *affect* the financial statements. (*Affect* is a verb.)

This change in accounting policy will have no *effect* on the financial statements. (*Effect* is usually a noun. Rarely, *effect* is a verb meaning "to cause to happen.")

The *cost* of the new machine is more than we expected. (*Cost* is singular.)

The *costs* of these assets are not recorded correctly. (*Costs* is plural, but when you say the word aloud, you cannot hear the final *s*.)

The ambiguous footnote may *mislead* investors. (*Mislead* is present or future tense.)

This ambiguous footnote *misled* investors. (*Misled* is past tense.)

How should we record the *principal* of this bond investment?

This procedure does not follow generally accepted accounting *principles.*

In summary, good grammar, punctuation, and spelling are essential for polished, professional writing. Don't just guess about the rules; resolve your uncertainties with a grammar handbook or dictionary. Remember the needs of your readers. Correct grammar and mechanics are necessary for smooth, clear reading.

A final word: It is important to proofread your finished product for typographical errors—whether you or someone else does the actual typing. Typing errors make work look sloppy, and the writer seem careless. Effective writing should look professional: correct, neat, and polished.

A word processor with a spelling check program will help you identify typographical errors as well as misspelled words. Review Chapter 2 for more suggestions on how to proofread effectively.

This chapter has given another rule for effective writing. We now have 17.

1. **Analyze the purpose of the writing and the needs of the readers.**
2. **Use an outline to organize the ideas you want to present.**
3. **Write the draft, and then revise it to make the writing polished and correct.**
4. **Make the writing unified—all sentences should relate to the main idea, either directly or indirectly. Eliminate digressions and irrelevant detail.**
5. **Use summary sentences and transitions to make your writing coherent.**
6. **Write in short paragraphs that begin with clear topic sentences.**
7. **Develop paragraphs by illustration, definition, detail, and appeals to authority.**
8. **Be concise—make every word count.**
9. **Keep it simple—simple vocabulary and short sentences.**
10. **Enliven sentences with active verbs and descriptive nouns.**
11. **Use jargon only when your readers understand it. Define technical terms when necessary.**
12. **Be precise—avoid ambiguous and confused meanings.**
13. **Be concrete—use facts, details, and examples.**
14. **Use active voice for most sentences.**
15. **Vary vocabulary, sentence lengths, and sentence structures. Read the writing aloud to hear how it sounds.**
16. **Write from the reader's point of view. Use tone to show courtesy and respect.**
17. **Proofread for grammar, punctuation, spelling, and typographical errors.**

EXERCISES

Exercise 5-1

Join these independent clauses together in three ways.

under variable costing a company's sales will influence income
under absorption costing both sales and production will affect income.

Exercise 5–2

Identify and correct fragments, comma splices, or fused sentences. Some sentences are correct.

1. Tinto Paint may argue that these costs do not provide future benefits, thus, Tinto may choose to expense them.
2. Ethel Corporation must not only improve its internal control system it must also review its procedures for accounts receivable.
3. Many types of users rely on financial statement information, for example, creditors use the information to evaluate a firm's credit worthiness.
4. Physical volume is one factor that affects cost behavior; other factors include efficiency, changes in technology, unit prices of inputs, etc.
5. The main reason for our concern, however, is the incorrect recording of accounts receivable.
6. Although, the reason for our decreased sales is not obvious.
7. The reason for our low inventory turnover being that this is our slow season.
8. Accountants do not depreciate land, therefore, we cannot allocate land costs on a systematic and rational basis.
9. Historical cost usually results from arms'-length transactions and therefore provides reliable measures of transactions.
10. Although we discussed this policy at the May meeting, some staff members still do not understand it.

Exercise 5–3

Some of these sentences have verb errors: subject-verb agreement or shifts in tense or mood. Identify these errors and correct the sentences.

1. Changes in the general purchasing power of the dollar forces accountants to deal with an unstable monetary unit.
2. If we improve our financial ratios, investors would find our stock more attractive.
3. Neither the president nor the supervisors understand the new policy.
4. One problem we found in our reviews of the records were that revenues were not always recorded in the proper period.
5. A statement with supplementary disclosures provide additional information to investors.
6. The physical flow of goods generally follow the FIFO pattern.
7. Each of these statements is prepared according to GAAP.
8. Neither the president nor the controller understand the new policy.
9. We will depreciate this asset over ten years. First, however, determine its salvage value.
10. The future benefits provided by the bond is partly due to its high interest rate.
11. Restating asset values to current costs results in realized and unrealized holding gains and losses.

12. We review the client's system of internal control. Then we will recommend ways to improve it.

Exercise 5-4

Correct any pronoun errors you find in the following sentences.

1. When an investor or creditor wishes to compare two companies, they cannot always rely on the historical cost statements for the comparison.
2. Ace Manufacturing should remember that they are allowed to expense the cost of certain property.
3. The FASB deals with research and development costs in their Statement No. 2.
4. Management is interested in improving the revenue figures for their report to the stockholders.
5. Each accountant is required to complete their report on time.
6. Although accountants often use reversing entries to reduce the possibilities of error, they are not essential parts of the accounting process.
7. The trouble with our new system is that you have so much trouble understanding it.
8. The Smallwood Corporation has greatly increased it's advertising expense.
9. A switch to LIFO usually results in a lower income tax liability and a lower inventory figure on the balance sheet; this would be important to our company.
10. The Board of Directors will hold its next meeting in July.
11. Every corporation coming under SEC regulations must follow certain procedures in preparing their financial statements.
12. Everyone registering for the convention will receive a package of information when they arrive.

Exercise 5-5

Revise the following sentences for parallel structure.

1. This committee will study the problem, a recommendation for correcting it, and oversee the correction procedures.
2. The hiring decisions will be based on three criteria: experience, training, and whether the applicants have good communication skills.
3. We recommend the following improvements in your system of internal controls:
   - The controls over cash should be strengthened.
   - An accounting manual to ensure that transctions are handled uniformly.
   - Improved documentation of accounting procedures.

Exercise 5-6

a. Complete the following chart.

Singular	Singular Possessive	Plural	Plural Possessive
statement			
company			
business			
cost			
risk			
CPA			
year			
industry			

    b. Use the words from the chart to fill in these sentences. The singular form of the correct word is given in the parentheses.

1. (CPA) _____ from all over the country will be at the convention.
2. (business) Investors examine a _____ statements to determine its financial condition.
3. (cost) Record all these _____ in the proper amounts.
4. (statement) Which of the _____ is in error?
5. (cost) What is the replacement _____ of this machine?
6. (risk) Investors in these bonds must accept certain _____.
7. (industry) Research and development are crucial in many _____.
8. (year) We should see a profit in two _____ time.
9. (company) The Board of Directors considered the _____ pension plan.
10. (statement) We are making changes in the two _____ totals.

Exercise 5–7

Punctuate the following sentences correctly.

1. When the Board of Directors met in December the company showed a net loss of $5,000,000.
2. To increase the revenues from its new product the company introduced an advertising campaign in New York Chicago and Los Angeles.
3. The biggest problem in our firm however is obsolete inventories.
4. We currently value our inventories according to LIFO not FIFO.
5. For example Elixir Products should consider FASB Statement No. 13 which deals with leases.
6. The auditors revealed several problems in Thompson Company's financial records such as its depreciation policy its handling of bad debts and its inventory accounting.
7. The presidents letter contained the following warning "If our revenues don't increase soon the plant may be forced to close"
8. "We're planning a new sales strategy" the manager wrote in reply.

9.   We have decided not to invest in the Allied bonds at this time instead we are considering Blackstone's common stocks.

10. Although our revenues increased during June expenses rose at an alarming rate.

Exercise 5–8

Identify and correct any misspelled words in the following list. Look up any words you are unsure of; not all of these words were included in the chapter.

1.   believe
2.   receive
3.   occured
4.   seperate
5.   accural
6.   benefitted
7.   existance
8.   principle (the rule)
9.   cost (plural)
10. mislead (past tense)
11. advise (the noun)
12. affect (the verb)

ANSWERS TO EXERCISES

Answers, Exercise 5–1

Under variable costing a company's sales will influence income; under absorption costing both sales and production will affect income.

Under variable costing a company's sales will influence income, but under absorption costing both sales and production will affect income.

Under variable costing a company's sales will influence income; however, under absorption costing both sales and production will affect income.

Answers, Exercise 5–2

NOTE: Some of the following errors can be corrected in more than one way. However, this key will give only one possible correction. If you recognize the error, you probably understand how to correct it.

1.   Comma splice. Correction:
     Tinto Paint may argue that these costs do not provide future benefits; thus, Tinto may choose to expense them.
                                    OR
     Tinto Paint may argue that these costs do not provide future benefits. Thus, Tinto may choose to expense them.

2. Fused sentence. Correction:
   Ethel Corporation must not only improve its internal control system; it must also review its procedures for accounts receivable.

3. Comma splice. Correction:
   Many types of users rely on financial statement information; for example, creditors use the information to evaluate a firm's credit worthiness.

4. Correct.

5. Correct. (*However* doesn't come between two independent clauses in this sentence.)

6. Fragment. Revision:
   However, the reason for our decreased sales is not obvious.

7. Fragment. Revision:
   The reason for our low inventory turnover is that this is our slow season.

8. Comma splice. Correction:
   Accountants do not depreciate land. Therefore, we cannot allocate land costs on a systematic and rational basis.

9. Correct. (*Therefore* doesn't come between two independent clauses.)

10. Correct. (The first clause—"although we discussed this policy at the May meeting,"—is not independent; it could not stand alone as a sentence.)

Answers, Exercise 5-3

1. Subject-verb agreement. Changes in the general purchasing power of the dollar *force* accounts to deal with an unstable monetary unit. (The verb should agree with the subject *changes.*)

2. Mood shift. If we improve our financial ratios, investors *will find* our stock more attractive.

   OR

   If we *improved* our ratios, investors would find our stock more attractive.
   (The original sentence contained a shift in mood from indicative to subjunctive. Either mood is correct here; the key is to be consistent.)

3. Correct.

4. Subject-verb agreement. One problem we found in our reviews of the records *was* that revenues were not always recorded in the proper period. (The verb should agree with *problem.*)

5. Subject-verb agreement. A statement with supplementary disclosures *provides* additional information to investors. (The verb should agree with *statement.*)

6. Subject-verb agreement. The physical flow of goods generally *follows* the FIFO pattern. (The verb should agree with *flow.*)

7. Correct.

8. Subject-verb agreement. Neither the president nor the controller *understands* the new policy. (The verb should agree with *controller.*)

9. Mood shift. We will depreciate this asset over 10 years. First, however, we *must determine* its salvage value. (The original sentence shifted from indicative to imperative mood.)

10. Subject-verb agreement. The future benefits provided by the bond *are* partly due to its high interest rate. (The verb should agree with *benefits.*)

11. Correct.

12. Tense shift. We *will review* the client's system of internal controls. Then we will recommend ways to improve it. (The original sentence contained a tense shift from present to future.)

Answers, Exercise 5–4

1. When an investor or creditor wishes to compare two companies, *he or she* cannot always rely on the historical cost statements for the companies. (Alternative: *investors or creditors/they*).
2. Ace Manufacturing should remember that *it* is allowed to expense the cost of certain property.
3. The FASB deals with research and development costs in *its* Statement No. 2.
4. Management is interested in improving the revenue figures for *its* report to the stockholders.
5. Each accountant is required to complete his or her report on time.
   OR
   All accountants are required to complete their reports on time.
6. Although accountants often use reversing entries to reduce the possibilities of error, these entries are not essential parts of the accounting process.
7. The trouble with our new system is that it is so hard to understand.
   OR
   The trouble with our new system is that I have so much trouble understanding it.
8. The Smallwood Corporation has greatly increased *its* advertising expense.
9. A switch to LIFO usually results in a lower income tax liability and a lower inventory figure on the balance sheet; these advantages would be important to our company.
10. Correct.
11. Every corporation coming under SEC regulations must follow certain procedures in preparing *its* financial statements.
12. Everyone registering for the convention will receive a package of information when he or she arrives.

Answers, Exercise 5–5

1. This committee will study the problem, recommend a way to correct it, and oversee the correction procedures.
   (The original sentence combined a verb phrase, a noun phrase, and a verb phrase.)
2. The hiring decisions will be based on three criteria: experience, training, and communication skills.
   (The original sentence combined a noun, a noun, and a dependent clause.)
3. We recommend the following improvements in your system of internal control:

   • stronger controls over cash
   • an accounting manual to ensure that transactions are handled uniformly
   • improved documentation of accounting procedures.

Answers, Exercise 5-6

a.

Singular	Singular Possessive	Plural	Plural Possessive
statement	statement's	statements	statements'
company	company's	companies	companies'
business	business's	businesses	businesses'
cost	cost's	costs	costs'
risk	risk's	risks	risks'
CPA	CPA's	CPAs or CPA's	CPAs'
year	year's	years	years'
industry	industry's	industries	industries'

b.

1. CPA's or CPAs
2. business's
3. costs
4. statements
5. cost
6. risks
7. industries
8. years'
9. company's
10. statements'

Answers, Exercise 5-7

1. When the Board of Directors met in December, the company showed a net loss of $5,000,000.
2. To increase the revenues from its new product, the company introduced an advertising campaign in New York, Chicago, and Los Angeles.
3. The biggest problem in our firm, however, is obsolete inventories.
4. We currently value our inventories according to LIFO, not FIFO.
5. For example, Elixir Products should consider FASB Statement No. 13, which deals with leases.
6. The auditors revealed several problems in Thompson Company's financial records, such as its depreciation policy, its handling of bad debts, and its inventory accounting.
7. The president's letter contained the following warning: "If our revenues don't increase soon, the plant may be forced to close."
8. "We're planning a new sales strategy," the manager wrote in reply.
9. We have decided not to invest in the Allied bonds at this time. Instead, we are considering Blackstone's common stocks. (Alternative: We have decided not to invest in the Allied bonds at this time; instead, we are considering Blackstone's common stocks.)
10. Although our revenues increased during June, expenses rose at an alarming rate.

Answers, Exercise 5–8

1. correct
2. correct
3. occurred
4. separate
5. accrual
6. benefited
7. existence
8. correct
9. costs
10. misled
11. advice
12. correct

NOTES

1. *Statement of Financial Accounting Standards No. 14: Financial Reporting for Segments of a Business Enterprise* (Stamford, Conn.: Financial Accounting Standards Board, 1976), para. 10a. Copyright by Financial Accounting Standards Board, High Ridge Park, Stamford, Connecticut, 06905, U.S.A. Reprinted with permission. Copies of the complete document are available from the FASB.
2. Ibid.

CHAPTER 6
Format for Clarity

How a document looks at first glance can make a big difference in how the reader reacts to it. An attractive document generally gets a positive response, but a paper which is not pleasing to the eye may never be read.

This chapter looks at techniques of document design that will make your letters, memos, and reports more attractive. But a good design will do more for the readers than appeal to them visually. A well-planned format will also contribute to the clarity of your documents by making them easier to read.

Later chapters will cover the conventions and formats specific to particular kinds of documents, such as the standard parts of a letter and the graphic illustrations of a formal report. The techniques covered in this chapter will be those you can use for any kind of document you write. We will consider ways to make your documents look professional and attractive, such as the choice of paper and print, and the use of white space. We will also see how techniques of formatting, such as headings and lists, can make your documents clearer and more readable.

A PROFESSIONAL APPEARANCE

A document with a professional appearance uses high-quality materials—the best paper and the best print. It incorporates an attractive use of margins and white space, and it is perfectly neat.

Paper and Print

Of course if you already work for a firm you will not have any choice about the paper; you will probably use your company's letterhead stationery and standard stock for all your documents. If you are still a student, however, you will need to select a paper that makes a good impression. Use $8\frac{1}{2} \times 11$-inch paper of a high quality bond, about 24-pound weight, in white or off-white. Never use erasable bond paper because it smears too easily.

The print of your document is another consideration. If you are using a word processor, you will need a letter-quality printer for a professional appearance. If you are using a typewriter, be sure that it produces a clean, even type. Electric typewriters usually turn out neater copy than manual machines do. And whether you use a typewriter or a printer, be sure to use a good ribbon.

A number of type styles are available on both typewriters and printers. Choose a standard type style, never a novelty style or one that simulates handwriting. The type size is also important. Most people find pica type easier to read than elite type because pica is a little larger.

White Space and Margins

White space is that part of a page which does not have any print. White space includes margins, the space between sections, and the space around graphic illustrations.

A document with visual appeal will have a good balance between print and white space. White space also makes a document easier to read. The space between sections, for example, helps the reader to see the paper's structure.

There are no hard-and-fast rules for margin widths or the number of lines between sections. As a general guideline, however, plan about a one-inch margin for the sides and bottoms of all your papers. The top of the first page should have about a two-inch margin; subsequent pages should have a one-inch margin at the top.

Leave an extra line space between the sections of your document. A double-spaced page, for example, would have three lines between sections.

For any document that is single spaced, be sure to double space between paragraphs.

Neatness Counts!

Whatever you write, the final copy should be error-free and extremely neat. Of course a word processor, especially one with a spelling checker, enables you to make corrections with ease. If you are using a typewriter, corrections should be few and unobtrusive. Sloppiness in a document seems unprofessional and careless.

FORMATTING

Some writers think of the format of their document only in terms of straight text: page after page of print unbroken by headings or other divisions. Yet if you look at almost any professional publication, including this handbook, you will see how various formatting devices, such as headings, lists, and set-off material, make pages look more attractive and easier to read.

Headings

For any document longer than a page, headings are useful to divide the paper into sections. Headings make a paper less intimidating to readers because the divisions break up the text into smaller chunks. In a sense, headings give readers a chance to pause and catch their breath.

Headings also help the readers by showing them the structure of the paper and what topics it will cover. In fact, many readers preview the contents of a document by skimming through it to read the headings. For this reason, it is important that headings be worded so that they indicate the contents of the section to follow. Sometimes headings suggest the main idea of the section, but they should clearly identify the topic discussed. If you look through this book, you will see how headings suggest the content of the chapters. Chapter 1 even uses questions for headings, which is a good technique if not overused.

Headings can be broken down into several levels of division. Some headings indicate major sections of a paper, while other headings indicate minor divisions. In other words, a paper may have both headings and subheadings. In this chapter, for example, "A Professional Appearance" (page 89) indicates a major section of the chapter; "Paper and Print" marks the beginning of a subtopic, because it is just one aspect of a document's appearance. Generally, a short document needs only one level of heading, but this rule can vary depending on what you are writing about.

The style of the heading, how the heading is placed and typed on the page, varies with the levels of division. Some styles indicate major headings; other styles indicate subheadings.

Here are four heading styles and the levels of division.

FIRST LEVEL: CENTERED, ALL CAPS

Second Level: Centered, Underlined

Third Level: Centered, Not Underlined

Fourth Level: Left Margin, Underlined

If you use fewer than four levels, your headings may be in any style, as long as they are in descending order. For example, you might use second-level headings for main topics and fourth-level headings for subtopics. Of course, if you are using only one level of headings, any style is acceptable.

It is possible to overuse headings. You would not, for example, put a heading for every paragraph.

Lists and Set-off Material

Another formatting technique that can make a document easier to read is set-off material, especially for lists. Mark each item on the list with a number, a "bullet," or some other marker. Double space before and after the list and between each item, but single space the items.

Here is an example using bullets:

Your firm might use data processing equipment in at least five additional areas:

- budgets
- payrolls
- fixed assets
- accounts payable
- accounts receivable

Set-off lists not only improve the appearance of the paper by providing more white space, but they may also be more readable. The following example presents the same information as straight text and in a list format. Which arrangement do you prefer?

Special journals increase our efficiency. They do this by providing a greater division of labor. Also, they cut down on the time needed to post transactions. Finally, they give us quick and easy access to important financial information.

Special journals increase our efficiency because they

- provide a greater division of labor
- reduce the time needed to post transactions
- give us easy access to important financial information

The letter on pages 105–106 shows other examples of set-off lists.

Occasionally you will use set-off material for other purposes besides lists. For example, long direct quotations are set off; they are indented and single spaced (see Chapter 5). Very rarely, you will set off a sentence or two for emphasis. Chapters 2–5 use this technique to emphasize the guidelines for effective writing.

Pagination

The final formatting technique we will discuss is a simple one, but it is overlooked surprisingly often. For every document longer than one page, be sure to include page numbers. They can be placed at either the top or the bottom of the page, be centered, or be placed in a corner. Begin numbering on page 2.

This chapter has completed the rules for effective writing.

1. **Analyze the purpose of the writing and the needs of the readers.**
2. **Use an outline to organize the ideas you want to present.**
3. **Write the draft, and then revise it to make the writing polished and correct.**
4. **Make the writing unified—all sentences should relate to the main idea, either directly or indirectly. Eliminate digressions and irrelevant detail.**
5. **Use summary sentences and transitions to make your writing coherent.**
6. **Write in short paragraphs that begin with clear topic sentences.**
7. **Develop paragraphs by illustration, definition, detail, and appeals to authority.**
8. **Be concise—make every word count.**
9. **Keep it simple—simple vocabulary and short sentences.**
10. **Enliven sentences with active verbs and descriptive nouns.**
11. **Use jargon only when your readers understand it. Define technical terms when necessary.**
12. **Be precise—avoid ambiguous and confused meanings.**
13. **Be concrete—use facts, details, and examples.**
14. **Use active voice for most sentences.**
15. **Vary vocabulary, sentence lengths, and sentence structures. Read the writing aloud to hear how it sounds.**
16. **Write from the reader's point of view. Use tone to show courtesy and respect.**
17. **Proofread for grammar, punctuation, spelling, and typographical errors.**
18. **Use formatting techniques to give your writing clarity and visual appeal.**

EXERCISE

Collect examples of effective and ineffective formatting—personal correspondence as well as professional publications.

CHAPTER 7
Letters

Accountants frequently need to write letters—to clients, government agencies, fellow professionals, and so on. They may write letters seeking data about a client's tax situation, for example, or information needed for an audit. They may also write letters to communicate the results of research into a technical accounting problem. Other typical letters written by accountants are engagement letters and management advisory letters.

For any letter to get the best results, of course, it must be well written.

This chapter will begin with some basic principles of good letter writing—organization, style, tone, and format. Then we will look at some of the typical kinds of letters accountants write.

BASIC PRINCIPLES OF
LETTER WRITING

Effective letters have many of the characteristics of other good writing—tight organization, correct grammar and mechanics, and an active, direct style. They should be, in other words, coherent, clear, and concise. Letters should also be neat and attractive.

Coherent Organization

Letters can vary in length from one paragraph to several pages, although many business letters are no longer than a page. But whatever the length, you should be certain about what you want to include before you begin; then you will not forget something important.

As with other writing tasks, you will need to analyze the purpose of your letter before you write it. If you are answering another person's letter, it will help to have that letter before you, and note any comments for which a reply is needed. Finally, jot down a brief outline to organize the material logically.

It is also important to think about who the reader of your letter will be, especially when you are writing about a technical topic. The knowledge and experience of your readers will determine how detailed the explanations of technical material will be.

Sometimes, for example, you will need to explain complex accounting procedures in words a nonaccountant could understand. Ray M. Sommerfeld and G. Fred Streuling, in their study *Tax Research Techniques,* have discussed user needs in writing letters to clients about tax problems:

> Like a good speaker, a good writer must know his audience before he begins. Because tax clients vary greatly in their own tax expertise, it is important to consider the technical sophistication of a client or his staff when composing a tax opinion letter. The style of a letter may range from a highly sophisticated format, which includes numerous technical explanations and citations, to a simple composition that utilizes only laymen's terms. In many situations, of course, the best solution lies somewhere between the two extremes.[1]*

Chapter 2 discusses purpose and audience analysis in more detail.

Like other kinds of writing, letters are organized into an introduction, a body, and a conclusion. Each section uses summary sentences to emphasize main ideas and help the reader follow the train of thought.

The *introduction* of a letter identifies the subject of the letter or the reason the letter was written. You may also need to mention previous communication on the subject, such as an earlier letter or phone call. The introduction should also summarize briefly the main ideas and/or recommendations discussed in your letter. If your letter is very long, it is also a good idea to identify in your introduction the main issues or topics the letter will cover.

The *body* of the letter is divided logically into discussions of each topic. Arrange the topics in descending order of importance: start with the most important issue and work your way down to the least important. Begin the discussion of each issue with a summary sentence stating the main idea or recommendation.

Paragraphs should be short, usually a maximum of four or five sentences, and each one should begin with a topic sentence.

The letter's *conclusion* may be a conventional courteous closing:

> Thank you very much for your help in this matter.

*Copyright © 1981 by the American Institute of Certified Public Accountants, Inc.

The conclusion is also a good place to tell your correspondent exactly what you want him or her to do, or what you will do to follow up on the subjects discussed in the letter:

> May I have an appointment to discuss this matter with you? I'll be in Chicago next week, October 7–12. I'll call your secretary to set up a time that is convenient for you.

If your letter is very long, your conclusion may also summarize your main ideas and recommendations.

Study the example letters later in this chapter to see how they are organized. For a further discussion of organization, see Chapter 3.

Conciseness and Clarity

Conciseness and clarity, qualities of all good writing, are particularly important in letters. You do not want to waste your readers' time, nor do you want them to miss your meaning. Come to the point quickly, and say it in a way they will be sure to understand.

A number of the techniques already presented in this handbook are useful in achieving short, clear letters. For example, you will want your writing to be unified—paragraphs with a central idea that is easy to spot. You will also want the letter to be as brief and simple as possible, while still conveying an unambiguous, precise meaning.

The techniques discussed in Chapter 4 show how to achieve a concise, readable writing style, one that will make your letters interesting, clear, and effective.

Tone

One of the most important characteristics of a well-written business letter is its tone, or the way it makes the reader feel. Chapter 4 discussed writing with the "you attitude," which means that you write from the point of view of your readers, emphasizing their interests and needs. Courtesy and respect are also important qualities of business letters—as, indeed, they are in all forms of communication.

In general, effective letters will reflect a personal, conversational tone. However, the best tone to use for a given letter depends to some extent on the purpose and reader of that letter. Review the discussion of tone in Chapter 4 to see how the content of your letter and your relationship with the reader can affect the tone you choose for your correspondence.

Form and Appearance

One of the primary characteristics of an effective letter is a neat appearance. Good stationery is important: 8½ × 11-inch, unlined paper of a high-quality bond, about 24-pound weight. Envelopes, 4×10 inches, should match the stationery.

Business letters should be typed, using a typewriter and ribbon that will produce a neat, clear copy, or printed on a letter-quality printer. If you must handwrite the letter, write legibly in black, blue, or blue-black ink. Corrections should be few and unobtrusive. Neatness is essential!

A letter is usually single spaced, with double spacing between paragraphs, although letters can be double spaced throughout (see the sample format on p. 98). Margins should be at least one inch on all sides and as even as possible, although the length of the letter will determine, in part, the margin width.

One-page letters should be placed so that the body of the letter, excluding the heading, is centered on the page or slightly above center. You may need to type a rough copy of the letter first and then adjust the size and placement of the margins to make them attractive.

A word processor makes it easy to experiment with margins and spacing until you get the best arrangement.

Study the diagram on page 98 (Figure 7–1). This diagram identifies the parts of a letter and their proper placement. Also review Chapter 6, which presents various formatting techniques that will add clarity and attractiveness to your letters.

Parts of the Letter

Heading. The heading contains your address (not your name) and the date of the letter. If you use letterhead stationery, center the date under the printed heading or place it next to the right margin.

Inside Address. The inside address is a reproduction of the address on the envelope. Place the title of the person to whom you are writing either on the same line as his or her name, or on the following line.

Anna M. Soper, President
Muffet Products
516 N. 25th Street
Edinburg, TX 78539

Anna M. Soper
Director of Personnel
Muffet Products
516 N. 25th Street
Edinburg, TX 78539

Try to address a letter to a specific person, rather than to an office or title. You can often find the name of the person to whom you are writing by phoning the company or organization.

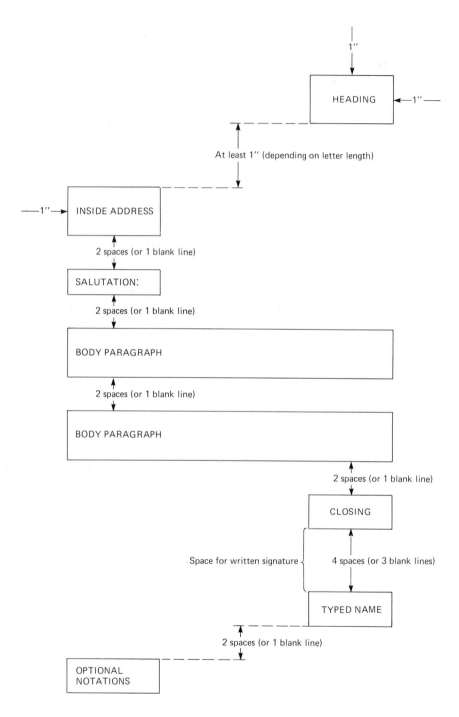

FIGURE 7-1. Diagram of a Letter Format.

Salutation. If possible, address your correspondent by name:

Dear Ms. Soper:

    or

Dear Mr. Smith:

For a woman correspondent, use *Ms.* if you don't know her marital status or if she prefers that title.

If you know your correspondent well, you may want to use his or her first name in the salutation:

Dear Anna:

Be careful with the use of first names, however, especially when you are writing to an older person or one in a higher position of authority than you are. In many situations, a respectful, courteous tone requires the use of a title and last name.

If you do not know the name of your correspondent, you can use a salutation such as the following:

Dear Director of Personnel:

Dear Sir or Madam:

Note that a colon (:) always follows the salutation.

Closing. The formal closing of a letter, which usually is placed next to the right margin, comes immediately above the signature. Capitalize the first word, and put a comma after the closing. Any of the following closings is correct.

Sincerely yours,

Sincerely,

Yours very truly,

Very truly yours,

Signature. Your name should be typed four lines below the closing; your position can be typed beneath your name. The space between the closing and typed name is for your handwritten signature.

Sincerely,

Anna M. Soper

Anna M. Soper
President

Optional Parts of a Letter.   Sometimes you will need additional notations below the signature, on the left margin. First, if someone else types your letter, a notation is made of your initials (all capital letters) and the typist's (all lower case).

> AMS:lc
>
> or
>
> AMS/lc

Second, if the letter includes an enclosure, make a notation.

> Enclosure(s)

Finally, if you will distribute copies of the letter to other people, note this fact.

> cc: John Jones

Second Page.   Many business letters are only one page long. If you need to write additional pages, each one should have a heading identifying the addressee, the date, and the page number. This information is usually typed at the left margin.

> Mr. Richard Smith
> November 18, 1989
> Page 3

RESPONDING TO CORRESPONDENCE

When you reply to a letter written by someone else, it is important to respond in a way that will build a good working relationship between you and your correspondent. Many of the techniques for effective letters already discussed apply to responses. Here is a summary of those techniques, as well as a few pointers that apply particularly when you are answering someone else's letter.

1. Respond promptly—by return mail if possible.
2. Reread carefully the letter you received, noting questions that need answers or ideas that need your comment.
3. For the opening paragraph:
    * Refer to earlier correspondence, such as the date of the letter you received.
    * If the letter is good news, or at least neutral, state clearly and positively the letter's main idea.
    * If the letter contains bad news, such as the denial of a request, identify the subject of the letter in the opening paragraph. State the explicit refusal later in the body of the letter, after you have prepared the reader with some buffer material.

4. Answer all your correspondent's questions fully and cover all relevant topics in sufficient detail. At the same time, your letter should be as concise as possible.

5. End with a courteous closing.

TYPICAL ACCOUNTING LETTERS

Before we begin this section, we should note that many accounting firms have standardized letters for some situations. For example, the management of a firm may have decided on the organization and even the specific wording that it requires its staff to use for engagement letters, management advisory letters, and the like. If your firm uses standardized letters, you will simply adapt the basic letter to the specific case you are concerned with, adding dates, names, figures, and other relevant facts.

Presented below are sample letters for various situations, along with some general comments on the content and organization of these letters.

Engagement Letters

Engagement letters put into writing the arrangements made between an accounting firm and a client. Engagement letters can confirm the arrangements for a variety of services—audit, review, compilation, management advisory services, or tax. The main advantage of an engagement letter is that it clarifies the mutual responsibilities of accountant and client, and thus prevents possible misunderstandings.

Engagement letters can vary a great deal in content, depending on the firm writing the letter, the type of services to be provided, and the facts of the case. However, W. Peter Van Son, Dan M. Guy, and S. Frank Betts have identified three basic elements of most engagement letters:

- a description of the nature and limitations of the service that the accountants will provide
- a description of the reports that the accounting firm expects to issue
- a statement that the engagement will possibly not disclose errors, irregularities, or illegal acts.[2]

In addition to these elements, an engagement letter may also include other information, such as important deadlines for the work; assistance that the client will provide, such as providing certain records and schedules; information about the fee; and a space for the client to indicate acceptance of the arrangements outlined in the engagement letter.

Page 102 (Figure 7–2) shows a sample engagement letter for an audit.

```
                        BROWN AND WYNNE
                    Certified Public Accountants

201 W. Tenth Street                              Austin, Texas 78712


                          July 15, 1989

Mr. George Smith, President
Heritage Manufacturing Company
301 Planters Road
Austin, Texas  78712

Dear Mr. Smith:

     This letter will confirm the arrangements we discussed for the
audit of Heritage Manufacturing Company for the year ended December
31, 1989.

     The purpose of the audit will be to examine Heritage Company's
financial statements for the year ended December 31, 1989.  Our
examination will be conducted in accordance with generally accepted
auditing standards, and we will use the tests and procedures necessary
to express an opinion on the fairness of the financial statements.
As part of our audit, we will review the internal control system
and conduct tests of transactions.  Although these procedures may
disclose material errors or illegal acts, a possibility remains
that we may not discover irregularities during the course of the
audit.

     At the close of our examination, we will issue our report on
the audit.  We will also prepare your federal and state income tax
returns for the year ended December 31, 1989.  Both the audit re-
port and the tax returns should be complete about March 15, 1990.

     Our fees will be at our reguluar rates, based on the time re-
quired to perform these services.  We will bill you when we have
completed the work.

     If you accept the arrangements outlined in this letter, please
indicate your acceptance by signing in the space below and sending
us the attached copy of this agreement.

     We are pleased that you have appointed us to be your auditor,
and we look forward to working with you and your staff.


                              Sincerely,

                              Carla Brown
                              Carla Brown, CPA

Accepted by:
Date:
```

FIGURE 7-2   Engagement Letter for An Audit.

Management Advisory Letters

At the conclusion of an audit, an accountant often writes a letter to the client suggesting ways the client can improve the business. This type of letter may contain suggestions on a variety of topics. For example, the letter may include recommendations for improving

- internal control
- the accounting and information system
- inventory control
- credit policies
- budgeting
- tax matters
- management of resources
- operating procedures

Sometimes, if the auditor includes many recommendations in the management letter, the letter may be quite long. If you write a management letter that is over three pages, consider organizing it into a report with a transmittal letter (see Chapter 9). Address the transmittal letter to the president or board of directors of the client's company, and summarize in the letter the major recommendations made in the report.

In any case, whether the management letter is a single document or a report with a transmittal letter, remember that long letters are more attractive and easier to read if they contain headings. These headings will divide the letter into logical sections.

Whatever the format of your management letter, write it so that it will be helpful to your client and build a good professional relationship between the client and your firm. The techniques for effective writing discussed so far in this book are certainly applicable to management letters: clear and logical organization, readable style, and specific and concrete explanations.

In an article in the *Journal of Accountancy,* Robert T. Lanz and S. Thomas Moser noted that management letters often anger clients because the letters don't give enough specific information to support the accountants' suggestions.[3] Lanz and Moser stress the importance of answering three questions about each recommendation:

- Why is the change needed?
- How can it be accomplished?
- What benefits will the client receive?

In addition, Lanz and Moser note that the letter should be well organized, with key points summarized near the beginning. The authors conclude their article with a brief discussion about the style of management letters:

Auditors may tend to write management letters in a perplexing combination of "legalese" and "accountantese." If this is what our clients are getting, we should put aside the technical jargon and verbosity and write a readable letter that makes good sense...[4]

An example of a short but effective management advisory letter appears on pages 105–106 (Figure 7–3). The recommendations included in this letter are taken from Lanz and Moser's article.[5]

Tax Research Letters

Accountants who provide tax services must often write letters to their clients communicating the results of the research into some tax question. These letters can be for after-the-fact or tax planning situations.

The content and organization of these letters can vary, but Sommerfeld and Streuling suggest the following basic outline:[6]*

- the facts on which the research was based
- warning that the advice is valid only for the facts previously outlined
- the tax questions implicit in these facts
- the conclusions, with the authoritative support for the conclusions
- areas of controversy that the IRS might dispute (Tax accountants do not all agree that the letter should identify the vulnerable areas in the client's situation. Sommerfeld and Streuling suggest that if the letter does identify these weaknesses, the accountant should caution the client to control access to the letter.)

In addition to a logical organization, such as the one outlined here, it is important that tax research letters be understandable to the client. Tax questions are often highly technical, and the accountant may need to explain the conclusions in terms a business person will understand. Read again the quotation on page 95 that emphasizes the importance of writing with specific readers in mind.

A sample letter reporting the results of tax research appears on pages 107–109 (Figure 7–4).[7]**

EXERCISES

Write letters for the situations described below. Use the proper format and effective organization and style. Invent any information you feel is necessary to make your letters complete.

Exercise 7–1 (all levels)

You are considering a move to a distant city, and you would like to work

*Copyright © 1981 by the American Institute of Certified Public Accountants, Inc.
**Copyright © 1981 by the American Institute of Certified Public Accountants, Inc.

```
                         BEASLEY AND POOLE
                     Certified Public Accountants
                          1553 W. Ellis Street
                       Atlanta, Georgia   30316


                           March 15, 1989


     Mr. Robert F. Freeman, President
     Southeast Manufacturing Company
     24 N. Broad Street
     Atlanta, Georgia   30327

     Dear Mr. Freeman:

         Our examination of Southeast Manufacturing's financial statements for
     the year ending December 31, 1988, revealed several areas where we believe
     you could improve your business:

         °  Adoption of data processing
         °  Stronger budgeting system
         °  Review of credit policies

     The following paragraphs will explain these recommendations in greater
     detail.

     Electronic Data Processing

     Due to the large volume of paperwork processed and the complexity of related
     transactions, the present manual accounting system has become unwieldy.
     In this connection, we suggest that consideration be given to using data
     processing equipment in the following areas:
     1.  Sales
     2.  Budgets
     3.  Inventories
     4.  Accounts receivable and cash receipts
     5.  Accounts payable and cash disbursements
     6.  Payrolls
     7.  Fixed assets
     8.  General ledger and journal entries

     Adoption of data processing in some or all of these areas would, we believe,
     reduce clerical workloads, tend to keep clerical salaries at a minimum
     and, most importantly, speed up bookkeeping functions in order to provide
     current financial information for management decisions and to facilitate
     the preparation of financial statements.
```

FIGURE 7-3   Management Advisory Letter.

Mr. Robert F. Freeman
March 15, 1989
Page 2

Budgets

Operating, selling and general administrative expenses for 1988 as compared
with 1987 increased from $1 million to $1,050,000, a change of 5 percent.
Although management has been able to control expenditures, we believe ef-
forts in this area would be assisted by implementation of a strong system
of budgeting.

Under such a system, responsibility for actual performance is assigned
to employees most directly responsible for the expenditures involved.
(It is best that such employees have a role in establishing the budgets.)
Periodic reports reflecting actual and budgeted amounts, together with
explanations of significant variances, should be provided to management
personnel responsible for approving the budgets initially. We cannot over-
emphasize the value of sound budgeting and planning in all areas of the
company's activities.

Credit Policies

The history of write-offs of bad accounts over the past few years indicates
that the write-off percentage has declined. Considering the low net earnings margin under which the company operates (slightly less than .6 percent
of net sales), it is most important that this favorable record continue
since a significant increase in bad debts could have a substantial negative
impact on net earnings.

In view of the high cost of money for business in general, management should
consider reviewing its credit policies to reasonably assure that the risk
inherent in continued sales to customers of questionable credit standing
is justified. This is a delicate area of policy; it is not desirable to
so restrict salesmen that profitable sales would be lost because of overly
stringent credit policies. However, a reasonable amount of control should
be exercised by the credit and collection department to assure a minimum
of bad accounts. For example, a limit could be set on the amount which
salesmen could extend to customers whose accounts have reached a certain
balance.

We will be glad to discuss these suggestions with you and help you
implement them.

Sincerely,

Roger Poole

Roger Poole
Beasley and Poole
Certified Public Accountants

FIGURE 7-3   Continued

ROBERT U. PARTNER & COMPANY
Certified Public Accountants
2010 Professional Tower
Calum City, U.S.A. 00001

December 23, 19X5

Mr. Red E. Ink, President
Ready, Incorporated
120 Publisher Lane
Calum City, USA 00002

Dear Mr. Ink:

This letter confirms the oral agreement of December 17, 19X5, in which
our firm agreed to undertake the preparation of federal income tax returns
for you and Ready, Inc., for the next year. The letter also reports the
preliminary results of our investigation into the tax consequences of the
incorporation of your printing business last March. We are pleased to
be of service to you and anticipate that our relationship will prove to
be mutually beneficial. Please feel free to call upon me at any time.

Before stating the preliminary results of our investigation into the
tax consequences of your incorporation transaction, I would like to restate
briefly all of the important facts as we understand them. Please review
this statement of facts very carefully. Our conclusions depend upon a
complete and accurate understanding of all of the facts. If any of the
following statements is either incorrect or incomplete, please call it
to my attention immediately, no matter how small or insignificant the difference may appear to be.

Our conclusions are based upon an understanding that on March 1, 19X5,
you exchanged all of the assets and liabilities of the printing business,
which you had operated for the prior twelve years as a sole proprietorship,
for 1,000 shares of common stock in Ready, Inc., a newly formed corporation.
The assets that you transferred to Ready, Inc., consisted of $20,000 cash;
$10,000 (estimated market value) supplies on hand; $50,000 (face value)
trade receivables; and $60,000 (book value) equipment. The equipment,
purchased new in 19X1 for $100,000, had been depreciated on a double-
declining-balance method for the past four years. An investment credit
was claimed in 19X1 on the purchase of the equipment. The liabilities
assumed by Ready, Inc., consisted of the $40,000 mortgage remaining from
the original equipment purchase in 19X1 and current trade payables of
$10,000. We further understand that Ready, Inc., plans to continue to
occupy the building leased by you on October 1, 19X3, from Branden Properties, until the expiration of that lease on September 30, 19X7. Finally,
we understand that Ready, Inc., has issued only 1,000 shares of common stock

FIGURE 7-4   A Letter Reporting the Results of Tax Research.

Red E. Ink
December 23, 19X5
Page 2

and that you retain 980 of those shares; that your wife, Neva, holds ten
shares; and that Tom Books, the corporate secretary-treasurer, holds the
remaining ten shares. The shares held by Mrs. Ink and Mr. Books were given
to them by you, as a gift, on March 1, 19X5.

Assuming that the preceding paragraph represents a complete and accurate statement of all of the facts pertinent to your incorporation transaction, we anticipate reporting that event as a wholly nontaxable transaction. In other words, neither you (individually) nor your corporation
will report any taxable income or loss solely because of your incorporation
of the printing business. Furthermore, no amount of investment credit
will have to be recaptured. However, in the future Ready, Inc. will be
restricted to a 150 percent declining-balance depreciation deduction on
the equipment transferred. The trade receivables collected by Ready, Inc.,
after March 1, 19X5, will be reported as the taxable income of the corporate
entity; collections made between January 1, 19X5, and February 28, 19X5,
will be considered part of your personal taxable income for 19X5.

If Ready, Inc.'s tax return is audited, there is a possibility that
the Internal Revenue Service may challenge the corporation's right to deduct
the $10,000 in trade payables it assumed from your proprietorship. If
you so desire, I would be pleased to explain this matter in detail. Perhaps
it would be desirable for Mr. Bent, you, and me to meet and review this
potential problem prior to our filing the corporate tax return.

If you wish to report the first corporate taxable income on a cash-
method fiscal-year basis, ending February 29, 19X6, it is imperative that
you have Mr. Tom Books keep the corporation's regular financial accounts
on that same basis. If he desires any help in maintaining those records,
we will be happy to assist him. It will be necessary for us to have access
to your personal financial records no later than March 1, 19X5, and to
your corporate records no later than April 15, 19X5, if the two federal
income tax returns are to be completed and filed on a timely basis.

Finally, may I suggest that we plan to have at least one more meeting
in my office sometime prior to February 28, 19X6, to discuss possible tax-
planning opportunities available to you in the new corporation. Among
other considerations, we should jointly review the possibility that you
may want to make a Subchapter S election, and that you may need to structure
executive compensation arrangements carefully and may wish to institute
a pension plan. It may be desirable to discuss these opportunities at
the same time that we meet with Mr. Bent to consider the question of

FIGURE 7-4   Continued

Red E. Ink
December 23, 19X5
Page 3

deducting the $10,000 in trade payables, as noted earlier. Please telephone
me to arrange an appointment if you would like to do this shortly after
the holidays.

Thank you again for selecting our firm for tax assistance. It is
very important that some of the material in this letter be kept confidential,
and we strongly recommend that you carefully control access to it at all
times. If you have any questions about any of the matters discussed, feel
free to request a more detailed explanation or drop by and review the complete files, which are available in my office. If I should not be available, my assistant, Fred Senior, would be happy to help you. We look for-
ward to serving you in the future.

Sincerely yours,

Robert U Partner

Robert U. Partner

FIGURE 7-4   Continued

with a local accounting firm there. You have five years' experience working as a CPA in the city where you now live.

Write a letter requesting an interview to discuss possible employment with the firm for which you wish to work.

Exercise 7-2 (all levels)

You have prepared the federal and state income tax returns for your client, Alexander Littleton. Write a cover letter to Mr. Littleton to mail with the completed returns. In your letter include:

- a reminder for him to sign the returns on the lines checked
- the amounts that he owes in both state and federal taxes
- a reminder of the filing deadline

Exercise 7-3 (all levels)

One of your clients, Alan Motors, has not paid for a tax return that you completed March 15, 1989. You billed Alan at the time you completed the return and mailed a reminder in May. At the end of June, Alan still hasn't paid the bill, and you need to write a letter to the company president, Mr. Roger Alan, requesting payment. Of course you do not want to antagonize Mr. Alan, because the company has been a client for several years and you value the business relationship.

Write the letter to Mr. Alan asking him to pay the bill.

Exercise 7-4 (all levels)

You are preparing the federal income tax returns for Mr. and Mrs. John Lapp and find you need some additional information: receipts for contributions to their church, the name of their youngest child, and the name of the day care center where the child is enrolled.

Write a letter to Mr. and Mrs. Lapp requesting this information.

Exercise 7-5
(Intermediate)

A friend of yours, Debbie Debit, has written you for advice. She tells you that she owns several shares of stock in Alpha Corporation. She has examined the most recent balance sheet of Alpha and has found that the common stock issued and outstanding totals 40,000 shares, and the market price per share is $25 on the balance sheet date. She is sure that the balance sheet is in error because, in her words, "the total assets are $1,100,000 and this current value should be the same as the total market value of the outstanding common stock."

In a letter, explain to your friend the various classifications of assets and how the "value" of each classification is determined to derive the "value" of the $1,100,000 in total assets. Also explain why the "values" of the assets and the stock are not the same.[8]

Exercise 7-6
(Intermediate)

One morning J. Worthington Pocketmoney stormed into the offices of Apple, Altos, and Monroe, his certified public accountants. Without waiting for the receptionist to announce his arrival, he entered the office of Samuel Andrews, the partner in charge of auditing Mr. Pocketmoney's home appliance store. As usual, Mr. Andrews listened politely and calmly to the monologue delivered by Mr. Pocketmoney. An edited version follows.

> This morning at my breakfast club I spoke with my competitor, F. Scott Wurlitzer. He boasted that his accountant had saved him $19,000 in income taxes last year by recommending a switch from the FIFO to the LIFO inventory flow assumption. If he can do that, why can't I? And why haven't you discussed this gimmick with me? I don't expect to rely on Wurlitzer for financial advice; I pay you for that.

After Pocketmoney's departure, Mr. Andrews calls you, a new staff accountant, into his office. He expresses regret at not having mentioned to Pocketmoney the possibility of a change in accounting method. However, he also advises you that Pocketmoney needs new capital in his business and is trying to interest another local businessperson in becoming a limited partner. Thus a decline in reported income could be detrimental to Mr. Pocketmoney's plans.

Mr. Andrews assigns you to draft a letter to Mr. Pocketmoney. The letter should provide a balanced discussion of the advantages and disadvantages of shifting from FIFO to LIFO, with particular reference to Mr. Pocketmoney's specific situation. Even though Andrews would like to provide some justification for his firm's failure to mention the possibility of a change, he cautions you to be reasonably objective and give adequate consideration to accounting theory.[9]

Exercise 7-7
(Intermediate)

Joel Barlow, the president of Marvel Cars, Inc., has sent you his firm's income statement, which is shown below. He has asked you to evaluate the statement and tell him of any shortcomings you find.

Write a letter to Mr. Barlow in which you discuss the problems you find with his firm's income statement as shown at the top of page 112.[10]

Exercise 7-8
(Intermediate)

Mr. and Mrs. Richard Webster want to invest in a deferred annuity for their son, Charles, who is ten years old. They want the annuity to pay exactly $10,000 a year for five years, beginning when Charles turns 21. They want to know how much money they will have to invest now, assuming the money will earn interest, compounded annually, of 8 percent.

Write a letter to Mr. and Mrs. Webster explaining deferred annuities and the amount they would need to invest now to set up the plan they have in mind.

MARVEL CARS, INC.
Statement of Profit and Loss
December 31, 1988

Revenues:		
Sales	$1,000,000	
Increase in market value of land and building	200,000	$1,200,000
Deduct expenses:		
Advertising	$100,000	
Sales commissions	50,000	
Utilities	20,000	
Wages	150,000	
Dividends	100,000	
Cost of cars purchased	700,000	1,120,000
Net profit		$ 80,000

Exercise 7–9
(Intermediate)

One of your clients is considering the implementation of a pension plan to cover the company's employees, some of whom have been with the company since it began operations eight years ago. Write a letter describing the issues involved in accounting for pensions without getting so involved with the technical details that your client, who has limited accounting knowledge, may not understand it.[11]

Exercise 7–10
(Intermediate)

You are a senior staff accountant with the firm of Taxum and Howe in Oberlin, Ohio. Your new client, Mr. Grabmore Gusto, would like your advice. Mr. Gusto is concerned about having audited financial statements for the first time this year.

To begin operations three years ago, Mr. Gusto invested $300,000 of his own money (his life savings) and borrowed $200,000 from Oberlin Bank and Trust. The loan carries a 10 percent interest rate and has a term of ten years from the date of issuance. Mr. Gusto set up a sinking fund immediately and has made monthly deposits to assure timely payments of interest and principal. Because of the success of his business, Mr. Gusto has been able to deposit enough money in three years to cover interest for the remaining seven years as well as the principal.

Mr. Gusto has recently developed a plan to expand his business, but needs to borrow about $500,000 to implement the plan. He is concerned, however, that Oberlin Bank and Trust will not grant him a new loan because of the existence of the original loan.

A business acquaintance, Mr. Suds, has suggested that because Mr. Gusto has deposited enough money in the sinking fund to cover principal and interest, he can simply eliminate both the sinking fund assets and the liability from his balance sheet. Mr. Suds referred to the elimination as debt defeasance.

Mr. Gusto is afraid that such an elimination or cancellation would not be in accordance with GAAP and would therefore result in a qualified audit opinion.

Write Mr. Gusto a letter explaining debt defeasance, including in your discussion a recommendation as to the conformity (or lack thereof) with GAAP.[12] He has researched the problem and is somewhat familiar with various applications and accounting treatments of defeasance.

Exercise 7-11
(Intermediate)

Suppose you were the CPA to whom the letter on pages 1114-115 (Figure 7-5) was written. How would you answer the letter?[13]

Exercise 7-12
(Auditing)

Write an engagement letter in which you agree to review the financial statements of Howard Fabricators, Inc. You may mention other services that you agree to provide.

Exercise 7-13
(Auditing)

One of your audit clients is Brown Manufacturing, which is owned by Charles Brown. Although your client has not discussed the problem with you, you have concluded that the business is in dire need of additional liquid funds. You have noted that payables are being liquidated well after discount dates have expired and that most equipment is being leased, rather than being purchased as is customary in most businesses of this type. The problem is being aggravated by a continued increase in volume, which has necessitated carrying larger inventories and receivables and leasing additional equipment at rates well in excess of normal depreciation charges and interest. The owner of the business has already invested all his available liquid funds in the business.[14]

Write a letter to Mr. Brown, suggesting ways he could improve the liquidity of his business.

Exercise 7-14
(Cost)

Evelyn Yale, president of Hotchkiss, Inc., your client, recently attended a seminar at which a speaker discussed planning and control of capital expenditures. The speaker referred to this approach as "capital budgeting." Yale tells you that she is not quite sure she understands this concept. Write a letter to explain the following topics:

1. Explain the nature and identify several uses of capital budgeting.

KEN—L—PRODUCTS, INC.
749 E. Peartree St.
Manhattan, Kansas 66502

May 1, 1989

Ellen Acker, CPA
331 J. M. Tull Street
Manhattan, KS 66502

Dear Ms. Acker:

As you well know, it is becoming impossible to conduct business without the constant threat of litigation. This year our company is faced with several lawsuits. We are unsure how these suits should be treated in our financial statements and would like clarification before you audit us this year.

Would you please specify the disclosure requirements for the following circumstances:

(1) Several show dog owners have filed a class-action suit concerning the product "Shampoodle." The plaintiffs claim that severe hair loss has occurred as a result of product use. The suit is for a total of $2 million. However, our attorneys claim that is is probable that we will have to pay only between $500,000 and $1 million.

(2) For quite sometime we have been producing a dog food called "Ken-L-Burgers." Recently we changed the formula and advertised the product as "better tasting." A consumer group known as "Spokesman for Dogs" has filed suit claiming that humans must actually eat the product in order to make the claim of better taste. Our lawyers say that the chance of losing this suit is remote. The suit is for $6 million.

(3) One of our workers lost a finger in the "Ken-L-Burger" machine. Our attorneys believe that we will probably lose this suit but are unsure about the amount.

(4) My brother's company, House of Cats, is being sued for $4 million. His lawyers say that it is remote that he will lose. However, Ken-L-Products, Inc. has guaranteed a debt he owes to a bank. If he loses, he will not be able to pay the bank.

FIGURE 7–5 A Letter from a Client. (Exercise 7–11.)

Ellen Acker
May 1, 1989
Page 2

      (5) A grain company sold us several tons of spoiled grain used as filler in our products. Since the company will not reimburse us for the spoilage, we have sued for $2 million. Our attorneys say we will probably win the case.

      (6) We aired several commercials that claimed Wayne Newton's dog uses our products. Mr. Newton told us that his dog hates our products and that if we show the commercials again he will probably sue us.

If each of these items is material, should we show them on the financial statements?

Thank you for your help on these disclosures.

Sincerely,

Ken L. Price

2. What are the basic differences between the payback (payout) method and the net present value method of capital budgeting? Explain.
3. Define "cost of capital."
4. Financial accounting data are not entirely suitable for use in capital budgeting. Explain.*

Exercise 7–15
(Auditing)

You have examined the financial statements of the Broadwall Corporation, a publicly held company, for the year ended December 31, 1987. Jack Elliot, President of Broadwall, has asked you to perform a limited review of the corporation's statements for the period ending March 31, 1988.

Write a letter to Mr. Elliot. Explain why your limited review will not provide a basis for the expression of an opinion.**

Exercise 7–16
(Advanced Managerial or Financial)

Assume one of the following situations:

1. You are a senior member of the auditing staff of a medium-sized manufacturing corporation.

OR

2. You are a partner of a regional accounting firm.

Write a letter to the Financial Accounting Standards Board in response to a recent FASB Exposure Draft.

Exercise 7–17
(Accounting Information Systems)

Parker's Shoe Store has been owned and managed by a very conservative individual who is intimidated by computers. The money from cash sales is kept in an old-fashioned cash register, and clerks keep track of the shoes sold by recording pertinent information (brand, style number, price, and size) on a yellow legal pad.

The owner of the store is planning to retire soon and his daughter, Sue Parker, will then be the full-time manager. She believes a computer system could help her run the store more efficiently, and she hires you to evaluate the store's needs and explain how a computer system could help her manage the business.

*Material from Uniform CPA Examinations and Unofficial Answers, Copyright © 1977 by the American Institute of Certified Public Accountants, Inc., is adapted with permission.

**Material from Uniform CPA Examinations and Unofficial Answers, Copyright © 1979 by the American Institute of Certified Public Accountants, Inc., is adapted with permission.

Write a letter to Ms. Parker explaining the benefits to the store of a computer system, as well as its limitations. Remember that while she is open-minded about the usefulness of computers, she knows very little about them.

Exercise 7-18
(Accounting Information Systems)

One of your clients, a small service business with ten office employees, plans to purchase a database package for use with the office's personal computers.

Select two database packages and evaluate them for your client's needs. Consider the advantages and disadvantages of both packages, including the ease with which the staff will be able to learn the new system. You should consider basic features of the database package as well as advanced functions.

Write your evaluation in the form of a letter to the company's president, Heather Owen.

Exercise 7-19
(Tax)

Elaine Harrison was divorced in 1988. Her unmarried daughter lived in her home for the entire year. It cost $6,000 to maintain her home in 1987, of which her former husband contributed $2,000 through support payments. Her former husband also provides more than half of their daughter's total support and claims her as a dependent under a written agreement with his ex-wife. What is Mrs. Harrison's correct filing status for the year?[15]

Write a letter to Mrs. Harrison in which you explain the answer to this question.

NOTES

1. Ray M. Sommerfeld and G. Fred Streuling, *Tax Research Techniques,* Studies in Federal Taxation No. 5 (New York: American Institute of Certified Public Accountants, 1976), p. 166.
    Sommerfeld and Streuling give additional information on other letters that tax accountants sometimes write: tax protest letters, requests for rulings, and determination letters.
2. W. Peter Van Son, Dan M. Guy, and J. Frank Betts, "Engagement Letters: What Practice Shows," *Journal of Accountancy,* 152, no. 6 (June 1982), p. 76.
3. Robert T. Lanz and S. Thomas Moser, "Improving Management Letters," *Journal of Accountancy,* 149, no. 3 (March 1980), pp. 39–42.
4. Ibid., p. 42.
5. Ibid., pp. 41–42.
6. Sommerfeld and Streuling, pp. 166–69.
7. Ibid., pp. 183–85.
8. Malcolm H. Lathan, "Writing Assignment for Intermediate Accounting" (unpublished class assignment, University of Georgia, 1982).

9. Randolph A. Shockley, "Writing Assignment for Intermediate Accounting" (unpublished class assignment, University of Georgia, 1982).

10. Charles Horngren, *Introduction to Financial Accounting,* 3rd ed., (Englewood Cliffs, N.J.: Prentice-Hall, Inc., © 1987), p. 67. Reprinted by permission.

11. Gordon S. May, "Writing Assignment for Intermediate Accounting" (unpublished class assignment, University of Georgia, 1987).

12. George Peek, "Writing Assignment for Intermediate Accounting" (unpublished class assignment, University of Georgia, 1986).

13. William R. Pasewark, "Writing Assignment for Intermediate Accounting" (unpublished class assignment, University of Georgia, 1987).

14. Adapted from Howard F. Stettler, *Auditing Principles: A Systems-Based Approach* (Englewood Cliffs, N.J.: Prentice-Hall, Inc., © 1982), pp. 667–68. Reprinted by permission.

15. Adapted from Prentice Hall, *1988 Federal Tax Course* (Englewood Cliffs, N.J.: Prentice-Hall, Inc., © 1987), p. 81. Reprinted by permission.

CHAPTER 8
Memos

Memos, also called memoranda or memorandums, are used for communication within an organization—between departments, for example, or between supervisor and staff. Memos may be of any length, from one sentence to several pages. They may be less formal than letters written to people outside the organization, but well-written memos have the same qualities as good letters: coherence, clarity, conciseness, and courtesy—all the techniques of the "you attitude." (See Chapters 4 and 7.)

This chapter will first discuss some of the general characteristics of effective memos. Then we will look at two special kinds of memos that accountants often write: memos to clients' files and memos that are part of working papers.

MEMOS: SOME
BASIC PRINCIPLES

Frequently memos are quite short—from one sentence, perhaps, to several paragraphs. The memo on page 120 (Figure 8-1) is an example. Notice the heading of the memo: the date, the person or persons addressed, the writer, and the subject. Frequently, as in this example, the writer's initials replace a formal signature.

Sometimes memos may be much longer than the one on page 120; in fact, they may be used for short reports. For longer memos, organization and structure are more complicated, so you will need to think of writing the memo in terms of the writing process discussed in Chapter 2. For example, you will need to spend some time planning your memo: analyzing its purpose, considering the needs and

```
                                    MEMO


        To:      All Employees

        From:    John Moore

        Subject: Ruth Morgan's Retirement Party

        Date:    June 5, 1989

                As many of you know, Ruth Morgan will be retiring next month after
        35 years on our accounting staff.
                We are planning a party in Ruth's honor on Friday, July 1.  The
        party will be at the Town Club from 5:00 PM to 7:00 PM.
                We hope everyone will be present to show Ruth our appreciation
        and best wishes.  Please let me know by June 23 if you and your spouse
        or friend will be able to attend.
```

FIGURE 8-1   A Short Memo.

interests of your readers, and finally organizing the material to be covered into a good outline. Once you have planned the memo, you can then draft and revise it using the techniques covered in Chapters 2–6.

The Parts of a Memo:
Organizing for Coherence

As with most kinds of writing, a memo is organized into an introduction, a body, and a conclusion. Summary sentences are used throughout the memo to make it more coherent. Study Chapter 3 again for a further discussion of the principles of organization that are reviewed here.

Introduction.   Most introductions are one paragraph long, although for a longer memo the introduction may be two or three short paragraphs. The introduction should identify what the memo is about and why it was written. If the memo will discuss more than one topic or be divided into several subtopics, the introduction should identify all the most important issues to be covered. For example, the introduction might contain a sentence such as the following to indicate the memo's contents:

This memo will explain how to account for patents, copyrights, and trademarks.

An introduction should also identify the main ideas and/or recommendations of your memo. Sometimes the main idea can be summarized in one or two sentences, but for longer memos, you may need an entire paragraph. If the summary of your main ideas is longer than a paragraph, it is often better to put it in a separate section immediately following the introduction. This section would have a heading such as "Summary" or "Recommendations."

Body.   The body of the memo is divided into sections, each with a heading that describes the contents of that section. Remember to begin by summarizing the main idea of the section.

A section may have one or many paragraphs. Paragraphs should usually be no more than four or five sentences long, and each should begin with a topic sentence.

Conclusion.   The conclusion of a memo may be very brief:

Let me know if you have any further questions about these procedures.

A conclusion such as this one brings the memo to a close, and ends in a courteous, helpful tone. It does not, however, summarize the main ideas of the memo.

How detailed to make a conclusion varies with the length and complexity of the memo. For long memos that cover complicated material, it is a good idea to summarize your main ideas and/or recommendations in the conclusion.

A conclusion is a good place to tell your readers what you want them to do, or what you will do, to follow up on the ideas discussed in the memo.

Concise, Clear, Readable Memos: Style and Tone

Memos should, of course, be as concise as possible: no unnecessary repetitions or digressions, and a style that avoids wordiness. They should be written in a clear, direct style, so that readers find them interesting and informative. Finally, memos should be flawless in grammar and mechanics.

Memos can vary considerably in tone, depending on what they are about and how they will be circulated. Some memos, such as the one on page 120, are quite informal. For these memos, a conversational, personal tone is appropriate.

Other memos are more formal, and may in fact serve as short reports. Some memos, such as those reporting the results of research or work performed, may become part of the permanent records in a client's file. These memos are usually written with a more impersonal, formal tone.

But whether formal or informal, all memos should be written in a vigorous, readable style. Chapter 4 explains and illustrates many techniques for giving your writing an effective style.

Finally, remember that techniques of formatting, such as headings and set-off lists, can add clarity and coherence to your writing. Review the formatting techniques discussed in Chapter 6, and then see how some of those techniques are used in the sample memos given in the remainder of this chapter.

SAMPLE MEMOS

The memo shown in Figure 8-2 was written in response to the hypothetical situation described below.

Situation:

Fred Lee is the proprietor of the firm for which you work. Mr. Lee wants to acquire a broadcasting business. The business he wants to acquire, DCL Broadcasting, is insisting that Fred pay not only for the identifiable net assets of the business, but also for something called "goodwill." Fred says to you: "What is this goodwill stuff? Should I pay for it or not? If I should pay for it, how much should I pay?"[1]

Study the memo on page 123[2] to see how it illustrates the principles of memo writing already discussed. Do you think Mr. Lee will be pleased with the memo? Why or why not?

Memos to Clients' Files

Sometimes accountants record information about a client's situation in a memo that is placed in the client's file for later reference. Other members of the staff may refer to the information recorded in these memos months or even years later, so it is important that the information be recorded clearly, accurately, and correctly.

For example, a client may write or call an accounting firm about a tax question. The person receiving the letter or handling the call will then write a memo to record the pertinent facts of the client's situation. Later, another member of the staff can research the question. The researcher will need adequate information to identify the issues, locate appropriate literature, and solve the client's problem.[3]*

A sample memo written for a client's file appears on page xxx (Figure 8-3).[4]**

Memos As Part of Working Papers

When accountants prepare working papers as part of their work on a case, they usually include memos summarizing the work they have performed, what they have observed, and the conclusion they have reached. In an audit, for example, the audit staff members prepare memos describing each major area of the audit. Then a supervisor, perhaps the auditor in charge or the engagement partner, will

---

*Copyright © 1981 by the American Institute of Certified Public Accountants, Inc.
**Copyright © 1981 by the American Institute of Certified Public Accountants, Inc.

MEMORANDUM   August 16, 1989

TO: FRED LEE

FROM: PETE WARDLAW

SUBJECT: PURCHASING DCL BROADCASTING

     This memo is in response to your questions concerning the purchase
of DCL Broadcasting. The memo will first explain goodwill and then
discuss how to determine its cost. I suggest computing the value of
goodwill to help determine DCL's maximum value. Thus, you would have
a dollar amount to help you determine how much you want to offer for
the company.

What Is Goodwill?

     Goodwill is an intangible asset made up of items that may contribute
to the value and earning power of a company. Some possible items that
may make up goodwill for DCL Broadcasting are

    1) High ratings
    2) Access to the most popular shows and movies
    3) Good managerial staff
    4) A large number of advertisers

These items increase the earnings of DCL Broadcasting, but they are
not listed on DCL's balance sheet. However, the amount of DCL's goodwill
should be included in the purchase price of the business.

Determining the Cost of Goodwill

     Excess cost over net assets and excess earnings are two ways to
determine the cost of goodwill. The first method computes goodwill
by subtracting the purchase price from the fair market value of DCL
Broadcasting's net assets. The second method uses DCL's past earnings
and the normal earnings of the broadcasting industry to compute estimated
excess earnings of DCL Broadcasting. Both methods will estimate goodwill
for DCL; however, I suggest using the excess earnings method because
it will allow you to see an estimated rate of return on your investment.
     Let me know if you have any further questions about goodwill or
the DCL acquistion.

FIGURE 8–2 A Memo.

```
                                                         October 30, 1987

    TO:       Files          R.
    FROM:     Tom Partner
    SUBJECT:  Potential exchange of common voting stock for preferred non-
              voting stock in Allemania Electronic, Inc.
                  Today, Tim Dietz, financial vice-president of Electric Supply Co.,
              called to request information concerning the tax consequences of a pro-
              posed recapitalization in Allemania Electronic, Inc., an 85-percent-
              owned subsidiary.
                  Allemania was acquired by Electric on June 1, 1987 and has been
              carried in the financial statements as a temporary investment on the
              equity basis.  The auditors of Electric (Meyerson, Garner and Leavitt)
              are now insisting that continued association with Allemania would require
              the inclusion of the subsidiary in Electric's financial statements on
              a fully consolidated basis.  The directors of Allemania are not in favor
              of such a disclosure and have suggested that Allemania exchange suffi-
              cient common voting stock for preferred nonvoting stock to reduce Elec-
              tric's ownership in the form of voting stock from 85 percent to 50 per-
              cent or below.  The board hopes, through the reduction of ownership
              in voting stock, that inclusion of Allemania on a consolidated financial
              basis with Electric can be avoided.
                  At the present time Electric and Allemania join in the filing of
              a consolidated tax return on a May 31, fiscal-year basis.  Responsibility
              for preparation and filing of the return rests with Electric's internal
              tax department, which we review on an annual basis.
                  Tim Dietz requested that our report reach him before Electric's
              next board meeting, which is scheduled for November 22, and he requested
              that we contact him personally for additional information.
```

FIGURE 8–3   A Memo to a Client's File.

often prepare a summary or review memo that includes comments on the entire audit process.

It is important that these memos be clear, accurate, and complete. Other members of the firm, or lawyers on either side of the court case who review the working papers later, may need to know exactly what procedures the auditors performed. Thus, these memos should be written in a direct, active style: "I [the person writing the memo] performed a cash receipts walk-through on May 31, 1989. I used admission ticket #51065 for the test."

The memo on page 125[5] (Figure 8–4) was written to record an inventory observation. This memo has a different organization and format from the sample memos given earlier in the chapter. Yet it surely illustrates the three qualities essential for effective writing: coherence, conciseness, and clarity. What specific techniques make this memo effective?

When your job requires you to write a memo, remember the techniques of effective writing stressed throughout this book. *Coherent* memos are logically organized and easy to follow; *concise* memos cover essential information in as few words as possible; and *clear* memos are precise, readable, and grammatically correct.

Prepared by: C.J.G. Date: 1/5/89
Reviewed by: A.C.E. Date: 1/11/89
F-3
Highlight Company
Inventory Observation Memorandum—Wayne Plant A
12/31/88

1. Observing clients' inventory taking. Four members of our audit staff arrived at the Wayne Plant at 7:40 A.M. on 12/31/88 for the inventory observation. All manufacturing and shipping operations had been shut down for the day. All materials had been neatly arranged, labeled and separated by type.

   Two teams of audit staff members each were assigned to different parts of the plant. Each team observed the care with which the client's personnel made the inventory counts and the control being exercised over the inventory count sheets. In every case, it appeared that the client's inventory instructions were being followed in a systematic and conscientious manner.

2. Making test counts. Each team made numerous test counts, which were recorded in our work papers (see F-2). The test counts covered approximately 22 percent of the inventory value and confirmed the accuracy of the client's counts.

3. Identifying obsolete and damaged goods. Each team made inquiries concerning obsolete, damaged, or slow-moving items. Based on our observations and inquiries, we have no reason to believe that any obsolete or damaged materials remained in inventory. We identified certain slow-moving items, portions of which on further investigation were excluded from the inventory (see F-4).

4. Observing cutoff controls. We observed that receiving reports were prepared on all goods received on the inventory date and recorded the number of the last receiving report prepared. No goods were shipped on 12/31. We recorded the number of the last shipping document used on 12/30. These numbers were subsequently used in our purchases and sales cutoff tests (see F-6 and F-7).

5. Conclusions. Based on our observation of the procedures followed by the client, it is my opinion that an accurate count was made of all goods on hand at 12/31/88 and that all obsolete, damaged, or slow-moving items were appropriately identified.

Carl Good
C.G.

FIGURE 8-4   A Memo As Part of Working Papers.

EXERCISES

Exercise 8–1
(All Levels)

You are newly hired as an accountant for the O-Y-Me Corporation, which is a small service business currently using the cash basis of accounting. The president of your company, Mr. Now U. Donit, has requested that you write a memo to him explaining what the accrual basis of accounting is, how it differs from the cash basis, and why O-Y-Me should switch from the cash basis to the accrual basis. [6]

Exercise 8–2
(All Levels)

You are controller of Carr Corporation. One morning you receive the memo in Figure 8-5 from the president of your company, Mr. W. R. Pasewark. Write a memo in response to the president's questions. [7]

Exercise 8–3
(Intermediate)

You are the controller of the Red Mesa Ranch and are preparing the ranch's financial statements for the year. You requested information from the cattle manager, Tuf Cowan, about the value of the ranch's livestock assets. Mr. Cowan sent you the memo in Figure 8-6, which asks you some questions about how to classify the livestock. Write a memo to answer Mr. Cowan's questions. [8]

Exercise 8–4
(Intermediate)

A friend of yours, Carl Credit, has come to you for advice. He has received an entry to the most recent Consumers Sweepstakes. He is puzzled over the prizes and the options available to him. A summary of the prizes follows:

Grand Prize:	$125,000 Cash
	or
	$ 20,000 per year for 10 years
First Prize:	$100,000 Cash
	or
	$ 24,000 per year for 6 years
Second Prize:	$ 80,000 Cash
	or
	$ 20,000 per year for 5 years
Third Prize:	$ 60,000 Cash
	or
	$ 18,000 per year for 4 years

CARR CORPORATION

OFFICE MEMO

To: I.N. Dunne, Controller

From: W.R. Pasewark, President

Date: June 26, 1989

Subject: Who sets the rules for accounting?

As you know, this will be the first year that our company has issued
audited financial statements. I am particularly concerned about what
rules we must follow in preparing our financial statements to accomodate
our external auditors.

Recently, I examined the audited financial statements of a company
similar to ours. The auditor's opinion section mentioned that the financial statements were prepared in accordance with "generally accepted
accounting principles." I suspect that these are the rules that we
must follow when preparing our own financial statements.

Would you please help me by answering the following questions concerning generally accepted accounting principles:

1. Who determines generally accepted accounting principles?
2. If we violate these rules, will be be breaking the law?
3. If these rules are not law, why must we follow them?

FIGURE 8-5   Memo for Exercise 8-2.

RED MESA RANCH

OFFICE MEMO

To: Ian Greenberg, Controller

From: Tuf Cowan, Cattle Manager

Date: June 28, 1989

Subject: Classification of livestock on the balance sheet

  I have received your request to value our livestock assets for the balance sheet for the year ending June 30, 1988. Based on available commodity prices, I can easily determine the dollar value of the livestock. However, I am unable to determine whether the following livestock categories should be shown as current items (inventory) or as long-term items:

1. Bulls--kept for breeding purposes; average useful life of ten years.

2. Steers--held for approximately 15 months from birth, then sold for slaughter.

3. Heifers--most kept for breeding purposes; a percentage of low quality or infertile heifers sold for slaughter.

4. Cows--used for breeding purposes; average useful life of five years, then sold for slaughter.

5. Calves--less than one year old, certain percentage sold as veal, others used for breeding or grazed and sold later for slaughter.

  Would you please assist me by specifying how I should classify each of these categories?

FIGURE 8-6 Memo for Exercise 8-3.

Carl knows that he will receive more total cash if he selects the periodic payments for each of the prizes, but he is afraid he is "missing" something in the offer (he does not understand present value principles).

In a memo, explain to Carl the time value of money. Also, advise him which settlement option for each of the prizes is better. (Carl must select the settlement options before submitting his entry.) Assume that payments are made at the beginning of each year and compute the interest rate at which Carl would be indifferent between the options. (You may present your calculations as a supporting exhibit to your memo and you may ignore income taxes.)[9]

Exercise 8-5
(Intermediate)

You have been hired as a special assistant to Sam Jones, the president of Bulldog Sales Company. Mr. Jones has little formal education, but is very astute about business matters and is an especially good salesperson. He calls you in and says, "Bulldog Sales Company is in the nice position of having excess cash on hand. I am considering investing that cash in some bonds issued five years ago by Red and Black Company, but I see in the *Wall Street Journal* that those bonds are selling at only 60 percent of their maturity value. Does that mean they are especially risky? Assuming I do make this investment, what are the accounting implications?"

Write a memo answering Mr. Jones's questions.[10]

Exercise 8-6
(Intermediate)

You are manager of the accounting department of Greenwood Sales Company, reporting directly to Joan Wilson, president. Ms. Wilson has little background in accounting, but is a very astute businessperson. She calls you in and says, "This year we spent $50,000 to count our inventory. This seems like a waste of money if the accountants are doing their job properly. Why do we need a count when your records should have this information?"

Prepare a memo that clearly answers Ms. Wilson's questions.[11]

Exercise 8-7
(Intermediate)

As a member of the technical staff of your CPA firm, you receive a request from a member of the audit staff for assistance in determining how to account for a large inventory of one of your clients. The company involved is a manufacturing firm that makes custom-designed machine parts. There are only two other companies in the country with the technology to produce these parts. Your client's firm is the largest of the three. Management has built a reputation not only in the quality of its products but also in customer service. One of the most successful policies it follows is always to manufacture a larger quantity of a part than a customer orders. The extra parts are kept in inventory so that if the customer later has an emergency need for the part, several may be shipped in a matter of two or three hours. The customers don't know that extra parts are being inventoried and therefore think that your client stops all other production to respond to the emergency. This greatly impresses customers and because of this, business has grown tremendously.

The problem is that any given customer will rarely, if ever, use this service. As a consequence, your client has built a huge inventory of production overruns, and only a small indeterminable amount of it is likely to be used. Your client does not show the inventory on the balance sheet because of its practice to expense the extra cost of production overruns as part of the cost of the production sold. A very large warehouse devoted entirely to this inventory is shown on the balance sheet, however, and is depreciated assuming a 20-year life.

Write a memo to Mr. Y. Doit of the audit staff stating your position on how to account for this inventory; deal with any other ramifications you may perceive. Your position should be formed after a *thorough* research of GAAP.[12]

Exercise 8–8
(Intermediate)

The following three independent sets of facts relate to (1) the possible accrual or (2) the possible disclosure by other means of a loss contingency.

Situation I
A company offers a one-year warranty for the product that it manufactures. A history of warranty claims has been compiled and the probable amount of claims related to sales for a given period can be determined.

Situation II
Subsequent to the date of a set of financial statements, but prior to the issuance of the financial statements, a company enters into a contract that will probably result in a significant loss to the company. The amount of the loss can be reasonably estimated.

Situation III
A company has adopted a policy of recording self-insurance for any possible losses resulting from injury to others by the company's vehicles. The premium for an insurance policy for the same risk from an independent insurance company would have an annual cost of $2,000. During the period covered by the financial statements, no accidents involving the company's vehicles resulted in injury to others.

Discuss the accrual and/or type of disclosure necessary (if any) and the reason(s) why such disclosure is appropriate for one of the three independent sets of facts above.*

Choose Situation I, II, or III. Prepare your answer in the form of a memo to the controller of the company for which you work.

Exercise 8–9
(Intermediate or Auditing)

Cranium Products Company manufactures a variety of sports headgear, which it sells to hundreds of distributors and retailers.

A company "cash clerk" processes all cash received in the mail (mostly checks from customers on account). He opens the mail, sending to the accounting department all accompanying letters and remittance advices that show the amounts received from each customer or other source. The letters and remittance advices are used by the accounting department for appropriate entries in the accounts. The clerk sends the currency and checks to another employee, who makes daily bank deposits but has no access to the accounting records. The monthly bank statements are reconciled by the accounting department, which has no access to cash or checks.

The sales manager has the authority for granting credit to customers for sales returns and allowances, and the credit manager has the authority for deciding when uncollectible accounts should be written off. However, a recent audit revealed that the cash clerk had forged the signatures of the sales manager and the credit manager to some forms authorizing sales allowances and bad debt write-offs for certain accounts. These forms were then sent to the accounting department, which entered them on the books and routinely posted them to customers' accounts.

How could the cash clerk have used these forgeries to cover an embezzlement by him? Assume there was no collusion with other employees. Be specific.[13]

Write a memo to the president of Cranium in which you discuss this situation.

Exercise 8–10
(Intermediate)

Milton Corporation entered into a lease arrangement with James Leasing Corporation for a certain machine. James's primary business is leasing and it is not a manufacturer or dealer. Milton will lease the machine for a period of three years, which is 50 percent of the machine's economic life. James will take possession of the machine at the end of the initial three-year lease and lease it to another, smaller company that does not need the most current version of the machine. Milton does not guarantee any residual value for the machine and will not purchase the machine at the end of the lease term.

*Material from Uniform CPA Examination Questions and Unofficial Answers, Copyright © 1977 by the American Institute of Certified Public Accountants, Inc., is adapted with permission.

Milton's incremental borrowing rate is 10 percent and the implicit rate in the lease is 8½ percent. Milton has no way of knowing the implicit rate used by James. Using either rate, the present value of the minimum lease payments is between 90 percent and 100 percent of the fair value of the machine at the date of the lease agreement.

Milton has agreed to pay all executory costs directly and no allowance for these costs is included in the lease payments.

James is reasonably certain that Milton will pay all lease payments, and, because Milton has agreed to pay all executory costs, there are no important uncertainties regarding costs to be incurred by James.

With respect to Milton (the lessee) answer the following:

1. What type of lease has been entered into? Explain the reason for your answer.
2. How should Milton compute the appropriate amount to be recorded for the lease or asset acquired?
3. What accounts will be created or affected by this transaction and how will the lease or asset and other costs related to the transaction be matched with earnings?
4. What disclosures must Milton make regarding this lease or asset?*

You are a staff accountant of the Milton Corporation. Write a memo to the controller, Helen Garcia, in which you answer these questions.

Exercise 8–11
(Cost)

A supplier to an automobile manufacturer has the following conversation with the manufacturer's purchasing manager:

> SUPPLIER: You did not predict the heavy demands. To keep up with your unforeseen demands over the coming quarter, we will have to work six days per week instead of five. Therefore, I want a price increase in the amount of the overtime premium that I must pay.
>
> MANUFACTURER: You have already recouped your fixed costs, so you are enjoying a hefty contribution margin on the sixth day. So quit complaining!

Should the supplier get an increase in price?[14] Write your answer in the form of a memo to the president of the automobile manufacturing firm.

Exercise 8–12
(Cost)

The Thomas Company is in the process of developing a revolutionary new product. A new division of the company was formed to develop, manufacture,

*Material from Uniform CPA Examination Questions and Unofficial Answers, Copyright © 1978 by the American Institute of Certified Public Accountants, Inc., is adapted with permission.

and market this new product. As of year end (December 31, 1988) the new product has not been manufactured for resale; however, a prototype unit was built and is in operation.

Throughout 1987 the new division incurred certain costs. These costs include design and engineering studies, prototype manufacturing costs, administrative expenses (including salaries of administrative personnel), and market research costs. In addition, approximately $500,000 in equipment (estimated useful life—10 years) was purchased for use in developing and manufacturing the new product. Approximately $200,000 of this equipment was built specifically for the design development of the new product; the remaining $300,000 of equipment was used to manufacture the preproduction prototype and will be used to manufacture the new product once it is in commercial production.

In accordance with Statement of Financial Accounting Standards No. 2, how should the various costs of Thomas described above be recorded on the financial statements for the year ended December 31, 1988?*

You are the controller of the Thomas Company. Write a memo to the president, Ruth Richards, in which you answer this question. Explain your answer in terms of SFAS No. 2.

Exercise 8–13
(Auditing)

A competent auditor has done a conscientious job of conducting an audit, but because of a clever fraud by management, a material fraud is included in the financial statements. The fraud, which is an overstatement of inventory, took place over several years, and it covered up the fact that the company's financial position was rapidly declining. The fraud was accidentally discovered in the latest audit by an unusually capable audit senior, and the SEC was immediately informed. Subsequent investigation indicated the company was actually near bankruptcy, and the value of the stock dropped from $26 per share to $1 in less than one month. Among the losing stockholders were pension funds, university endowment funds, retired couples, and widows. The individuals responsible for perpetrating the fraud were also bankrupt.

After making an extensive investigation of the audit performance in previous years, the SEC was satisfied that the auditor had done a high-quality audit and had followed generally accepted auditing standards in every respect. The commission concluded that it would be unreasonable to expect auditors to uncover this type of fraud.

State your opinion about who should bear the loss of the management fraud. Include in your discussion a list of potential bearers of the loss, and state why you believe they should or should not bear the loss.[15]

*Material from Uniform CPA Examination Questions and Unofficial Answers, Copyright © 1978 by the American Institute of Certified Public Accountants, Inc., is adapted with permission.

Write your discussion in the form of a memo to a partner in your firm.

Exercise 8–14
(Auditing)

As part of the analytical review of Mahogany Products, Inc., you perform calculations of the following ratios:

Ratio	Industry Averages 1988	1987	Mahogany Products 1988	1987
1. Current ratio	3.30	3.80	2.20	2.60
2. Days to collect receivables	87.00	93.00	67.00	60.00
3. Days to sell inventory	126.00	121.00	93.00	89.00
4. Purchases—accounts payable	11.70	11.60	8.50	8.60
5. Inventory—current assets	.56	.51	.49	.48
6. Operating earnings—tangible assets	.08	.06	.14	.12
7. Operating earnings—net sales	.06	.06	.04	.04
8. Gross margin percent	.21	.27	.21	.19
9. Earnings per share	$14.27	$13.91	$2.09	$1.93

For each of the ratios above:

1. State whether there is a need to investigate the results further and, if so, the reason for further investigation.
2. State the approach you would use in the investigation.
3. Explain how the operations of Mahogany Products appear to differ from those of the industry.[16]

Write your answers in the form of a memo to the auditor in charge of this review.

Exercise 8–15
(Accounting Information Systems)

You are a new accountant on the staff of Walker Manufacturing. Walker has been on a manual accounting system, but now plans to convert to a computerized system.

The president of the company, Roland Walker, knows that there are several methods a company can use to convert from a manual to an automated system, but he does not know which method would be better for his company.

Write a memo to the president in which you compare the four methods of conversion, and recommend the best one for Walker Manufacturing.

Exercise 8–16
(Accounting Information Systems)

For many CPA firms, in-house tax preparation gives higher profitability and increased control. It may also lead to staff and client frustration if procedural nightmares or equipment inadequacies interfere with return preparation. A rule of thumb is that a firm preparing more than 200 returns a year could be more profitable with in-house rather than service bureau tax return preparation. This informal guide may not apply, however, in all cases.

Progresso and Progresso, CPAs, have asked you, their most knowledgeable systems staff member, to investigate in-house tax preparation from two viewpoints: (1) differential costs and (2) procedural changes. Managing Partner I. M. Progresso thinks the firm could process 60 percent of the returns in-house initially and reach 95 percent by the third year. Some data relevant to your study are:

Number of original returns next year (estimated)	200
Number of returns corrected next year (estimated)	80
Average service bureau cost per return (original and corrected)	$45
Purchase price of tax preparation software	$5,500
Annual software license renewal	$2,600
PC hardware cost per year (capacity of 700 returns)	$5,300
Key input cost per return: original	$4
Key input cost per return: corrected	$1
Supply cost per return printed	$1
Tax practice growth rate per year	20%

Write a memo to I. M. Progresso recommending whether to bring tax preparation in-house. Justify your recommendation on the basis of cost analyses and significant qualitative aspects of changed procedures.[17]

Exercise 8–17
(Tax)

Mark Rood has asked you to prepare his income tax return for the tax year ending December 31, 1988. His records indicate that he received wages and commissions of $30,000 from his job as a salesperson. The records also indicate that Rood did the following during the year:

1. Transferred one-half of his 100 shares of IMP stock, bought in 1986 for $12 a share and worth (on the date of the transfer) $26 a share, to his divorced wife as part of their property settlement.
2. Sold 50 shares of the IMP stock in March of 1988 for $29 a share.

3. Bought a rare Mongolian coin to add to his collection in March of 1988 for $1,000. In August, he sold the coin for $1,800.

4. Bought a Ghanian coin for $2,500 in September and sold it in November for $1,000.

Assuming these are Rood's only capital assets transactions during the year, what is his adjusted gross income?

Write a memo to Rood's file in which you answer this question. Be sure to show the step-by-step computation of his gains and losses.[18]

Exercise 8-18
(Tax)

The George Valentine Company's current earnings and profits were $2,000,000 during the year. Has the company made a distribution of taxable dividends in any of the following transactions? Explain.

1. The company owns and rents a luxury apartment building. It rents one of its 5-room apartments to its major stockholder at 30 percent less than its fair rental value.

2. The company loans $80,000 to its 50 percent shareholder to help him buy a home. In return, the shareholder gives the company a personal note as security for the loan and is charged a reasonable rate of interest (equivalent to the applicable federal rate). The company carries the loan on its books as an account receivable.

3. Mr. George Valentine was the founder and the former chairman of the board of the company. He retired 10 years ago, having been adequately compensated during the years of his active service. He still owns 100 percent of the company stock. He was paid a fee of $100,000 this year even though he had not been active in business since his retirement.

Write a memo to the client file of the George Valentine Company. Analyze each transaction, and explain why it is or is not a distribution of taxable dividends.[19]

NOTES

1. Thomas M. Barton, "Writing Assignment for Intermediate Accounting" (unpublished class assignment, University of Georgia, 1987).

2. Pete Wardlaw, "Purchasing DCL Broadcasting" (unpublished student paper, University of Georgia, 1987).

3. Ray M. Sommerfeld and G. Fred Streuling, *Tax Research Techniques,* Studies in Federal Taxation No. 5 (New York: American Institute of Certified Public Accountants, 1976), p. 162.

4. Adapted from Sommerfeld and Streuling, p. 163.

5. Reprinted by permission, from pp. 490–491 in *Modern Auditing* by Walter G. Kell and Richard E. Ziegler. Copyright © 1980 by John Wiley & Sons, Inc.

6. Gordon S. May, "Writing Assignment for Intermediate Accounting" (unpublished class assignment, University of Georgia, 1987).

7. William R. Pasewark, "Writing Assignment for Intermediate Accounting" (unpublished class assignment, University of Georgia, 1987).

8. Ibid.
9. Malcolm H. Lathan, "Writing Assignment for Intermediate Accounting" (unpublished class assignment, University of Georgia, 1982).
10. Gadis J. Dillon, "Writing Assignment for Intermediate Accounting" (unpublished class assignment, University of Georgia, 1982).
11. Ibid.
12. Gordon S. May, "Writing Assignment for Intermediate Accounting" (unpublished class assignment, University of Georgia, 1982).
13. Charles T. Horngren, *Introduction to Financial Accounting* (Englewood Cliffs, N.J.: Prentice-Hall, Inc., © 1981), p. 336. Reprinted by permission.
14. Charles T. Horngren, *Introduction to Management Accounting,* 5th edition (Englewood Cliffs, N.J.: Prentice-Hall, Inc., © 1981), p. 110. Reprinted by permission.
15. Alvin A. Arens and James K. Loebbecke, *Auditing: An Integrated Approach,* 3rd edition (Englewood Cliffs, N.J.: Prentice-Hall, Inc., © 1984), pp. 157–58. Reprinted by permission.
16. Ibid., pp. 225–26.
17. Fay Borthick, "Writing Assignment" (unpublished class assignment, University of Tennessee, 1987).
18. Adapted from Prentice Hall, *1988 Federal Tax Course* (Englewood Cliffs, N.J.: Prentice-Hall, Inc., © 1987), p. 162. Reprinted by permission.
19. Ibid., p. 279.

CHAPTER 9
Reports

.

In some situations accountants may need to prepare formal reports. A CPA, for example, may prepare a report for a client. Mangerial accountants may prepare a report for another department within their firm or perhaps for a group of managers with a particular need. A report usually involves analysis of an accounting problem and application of accounting principles to a particular situation. It may also require some research of the professional literature or other material, so the research techniques discussed in Chapter 11 are often part of a report's preparation.

Reports will vary in length, but all reports should meet certain basic criteria. The accounting content should be accurate, the organization should be coherent, the report should be presented attractively, and the writing style should be clear and concise.

PLANNING A REPORT

The analysis of a report's purpose and audience may be more difficult than it is for letters and memos. A report may have many groups of readers, and each group will have different interests and needs.

For example, a report recommending that a firm invest in a new computer system might be circulated to the MIS department, the accounting department, the various departments that would actually use the system, and senior management. The accounting department would, of course, be interested in the accounting aspects of the acquisition as well as how the system could be used for various accounting tasks. The MIS department would be interested in the technical features of the system and how it would affect MIS personnel. Other departments would want to know how the system would make their work easier or more difficult, whether it would affect their budgets, and whether their personnel would have the training to use the system. Senior management, on the other hand, would be interested in a bigger picture, such as how the system would affect the firm's efficiency, competitiveness, and cash flow.

If you were writing this report, you would need to identify clearly who the readers would be and what information they would want the report to include. You would obviously be writing to readers with different degrees of knowledge about the technical aspects of the new system and with different interests and concerns as well. The way to handle this complicated situation is to write different parts of the report for different groups of readers.

Fortunately, many reports are not as difficult to plan and write as this one would be. But this example shows how important it is to analyze carefully the purposes and readers of the report when you are planning its contents.

Most reports require a great deal of research. They may report the results of empirical studies or pilot projects, or report research involving technical literature or generally accepted accounting principles. Organizing this research into a coherent outline is essential. Review the principles of organization discussed in Chapter 3, and then apply the following questions to your report as you are planning the outline and structuring your draft.

1. Is the subject covered adequately?
   * background information when necessary
   * adequate explanations, supporting data, and examples
   * citations from GAAP and other authorities, as needed
   * application to the specific needs and interests of readers
2. Is the report too long?
   * digressions—off the subject
   * too much explanation or detail
   * repetitions or wordiness
3. Is the report organized logically?
   * an order from most to least important
   * summary sentences where helpful
   * transitions to link ideas
   * short, well-organized paragraphs with topic sentences

The format of a report, how its various parts are put together, will also make it more coherent.

THE PARTS OF A REPORT

There are a variety of report formats, but they are all designed to make the report easy to read. The format presented in this handbook is typical of the ways in which reports are structured.

A report may include the following parts:

transmittal document
title page
table of contents
list of illustrations
summary section
introduction
body of the report
conclusion
appendices
notes
bibliography

Transmittal Document

The transmittal document can be either a letter or memo, depending on whether you are sending your report to someone outside your organization or within it. This document serves as a cover letter or memo: it presents the report to the people for whom it was written and adds any other information that will be helpful.

The transmittal document will not be long, but it should include some essential information: the report's title, what it is about , and why it was written. It is usually a good idea to summarize the main idea or recommendation of the report, if you can do so in about one or two sentences. You may want to add other comments about the report that will be helpful to the readers, but always end with a courteous closing.

Whereas the style of the actual report is usually formal and impersonal (see page 144), the transmittal document can usually be more conversational, including the use of personal pronouns.

Title Page

In a report prepared in a professional situation, the title page may look something like this:

Title of Report
Prepared by. . .
Prepared for. . .
Date

In a student report, more information is helpful.

Title of Report
Student's Name
Course and Period
Instructor
Date

Table of Contents

The table of contents should be on a separate page and should have a heading. The contents listed will be the major parts of the report, excluding the transmittal document, with the appropriate page numbers.

List of Illustrations

The list of illustrations, if applicable, will include titles and page numbers of graphs, charts, and other illustrations.

Summary Section

All formal reports should have a section at the beginning of the report that summarizes the main ideas and recommendations. This section can vary in length from one paragraph to several pages, and it can come either immediately before or immediately after the introduction. The summary section may be called an executive summary, abstract, synopsis, summary, or some other term.

An executive summary is especially helpful for long reports. This section gives the readers an overview of the report's contents without the technical detail. Busy managers may read the executive summary to decide whether they should read the entire report.

The executive summary will identify the purpose and scope of the report and possibly the methods used for research. It will include the major findings of the research, the conclusions of the researcher, and the recommendations.

The length of an executive summary will vary with the length of the report, but it is generally about one to three double-spaced pages. It should begin on a separate page following the table of contents or list of illustrations, and should be entitled *Executive Summary.*

For shorter reports, a section right after the introduction can provide a summary of the report's main ideas and recommendations. This section should be labeled *Summary;* it will be one or two paragraphs long. The sample report at the end of this chapter uses this kind of summary.

Introduction

The introduction of a formal report is longer than that for a letter or memo.

It will probably be at least two or three short paragraphs, and for long reports may even be longer than a page.

The introduction should identify the subject of the report and may state why it was written—who requested or authorized it, or for whom it was prepared. The introduction should state the purpose of the report in specific terms:

> The purpose of this report is to discuss the feasibility of offering a stock bonus plan to employees of Greenpine Industries.
>
> NOT: The purpose of this report is to discuss stock bonus plans.

Sometimes the introduction will include additional information to help the reader. It may, for example, give a brief background of the report's topic. However, if it is necessary to include very much background information, this material should be presented in a separate section within the body of the report.

Finally, the introduction of a report should end with a plan of development that gives the reader an overview of the topics the report will cover in the order they will be presented. A simple plan of development may be in sentence form.

> This report will describe the proposed pension plan and then discuss its costs and benefits.

However, sometimes a set-off list makes the plan of development easier to read:

> This report will discuss the following topics related to the proposed pension plan:
> 1. Major provisions
> 2. Benefits to employees
> 3. Benefits to the corporation
> 4. Cost
> 5. Accounting for the plan

Body of the Report

The body of the report should be divided into sections and possibly subsections, each with an appropriate heading. (Chapter 6 discusses headings.) Remember to begin each section with a statement that summarizes the main idea to be covered in that section.

Conclusion

In addition to the summary section at the beginning, a report should have a conclusion to remind the reader of the report's main ideas and conclusions. Depending on the length of the report, the conclusion may be from one paragraph to several pages.

Appendices (optional)

Depending on the report's audience and purpose, you may want to place highly technical information, statistics, etc., in appendices at the end of the report. If you use an appendix, give it a title and refer to it in the body of the report.

End Matter

What to put at the end of the report depends in part on the style of documentation you use (see Chapter 11). If you use endnotes, they should begin on a separate page and be labeled *Notes*.

Almost all reports will have some sort of bibliography or reference list. This list will identify the sources you cited within your paper, and it may also include additional references that the reader might wish to consult. This section should begin on a separate page following the notes (if any), and should have a title such as *Bibliography* or *References*.

Chapter 11 demonstrates the proper form for endnotes and bibliographical entries.

Graphic Illustrations

Graphic illustrations, such as tables, charts, or graphs, can sometimes make a report more interesting and informative. Tables or charts are an efficient way to present and summarize numerical data, and graphs are useful for comparisons. Software packages are available that produce graphics that look professional.

If you include graphics, number them and give them a descriptive title. Graphic illustrations should be labeled sufficiently so that they are self-explanatory, but they should also be discussed within the text of the report. This discussion should refer to the illustration by name and number (for example, Table 1). The discussion should appear in the text before the illustration.

If you are using an illustration with a lot of numbers, you may need to use a highlighting technique, such as bold face type, to make the most significant figures stand out.

Graphic illustrations can be placed either in the body of your report, close to the place in the text where they are discussed, or in an appendix.

APPEARANCE

It is important to present your report as attractively as possible. Use good quality paper and be sure that the report is neatly typed or printed. Corrections should be few and unobtrusive.

Reports should be double-spaced, with the exception of the transmittal document and any set-off material. Pages should be numbered, using lower case Roman numerals for prefatory pages (table of contents, list of illustrations, executive summary) and Arabic numerals for the remainder of the report, from the introduction through the end matter.

STYLE AND TONE

The tone of a formal report should usually be just what its names implies—formal, and therefore impersonal. You probably would not, for example, use personal pronouns, contractions, or a conversational style.

However, a formal style should still be readable and interesting, so you should use the techniques of effective style discussed in Chapter 4. Even a formal document can be written simply, clearly, and concretely.

In contrast with the actual report, the transmittal document may be written in a personal, conversational style.

The report beginning on page 145 (Figure 9–1) illustrates many of these techniques of effective report writing.[1]

EXERCISES

Write reports for the following situations. Invent any details you need to make the reports complete.

Exercise 9–1
(Intermediate)

You have received an inquiry from a prospective client, Johnson Marketing, Inc., concerning the accounting for inventories. Johnson is in the process of establishing a very large mail order business that will require a large inventory of miscellaneous items to be sold at different markups. Write a report for this client explaining briefly the various options of accounting for inventories and their effects. Remember that your client is *not* an accountant and knows very little about accounting.[2]

Exercise 9–2
(Intermediate)

Smith and Jones are planning to open a new downtown shoe store. Smith has heard of the FIFO, LIFO, specific identification, and lower-of-cost-or-market methods of valuing inventory, but does not understand them. Since you will be the accountant for the partnership, Smith has asked you to prepare a report recommending an appropriate method for valuing the inventory. Jones has asked that the report describe the advantages and disadvantages of each method, from both practical and theoretical perspectives.[3]

Exercise 9–3
(Intermediate)

Southeastern Enterprises, an association of real estate developers, has contacted your firm. The association is interested in your position on the recognition

```
                                              125 Easy Street
                                              Athens, Georgia
                                              August 8, 1989


Mr. John Ehrlich
Zealous Corporation
1890 Monroe Drive
Atlanta, Georgia  30306

Dear Mr. Ehrlich:

     As you requested in your letter of July 21, I have assembled infor-
mation about convertible debt to help you in your financing decision.
The accompanying report, entitled Financial and Accounting Considerations
in Issuing Convertible Debt, examines the nature of convertible debt,
the pros and cons of such an issue, and the accounting treatment of
the securities.

     As you suggested, I have discussed the accounting standards (GAAP)
affecting convertible debt.  Two Opinions of the Accounting Principles
Board, Nos. 14 and 15, have particular bearing on convertible debt;
each is logical, but the logic of one is quite inconsistent with the
logic of the other.

     I believe that you will find the standards interesting, and I hope
that my report will meet your needs.


                                              Sincerely yours,


                                              Jean Bryan
                                              Jean Bryan



jhw
```

FIGURE 9-1   A Report

FINANCIAL AND ACCOUNTING CONSIDERATIONS
OF ISSUING CONVERTIBLE DEBT

BY

JEAN BRYAN

ACCOUNTING 501
PERIOD 3-4, M-W

DR. ENGSTROM

AUGUST 8, 1989

FIGURE 9-1 Continued

CONTENTS

FIGURE 9-1 Continued

FINANCIAL AND ACCOUNTING CONSIDERATIONS OF ISSUING CONVERTIBLE DEBT

INTRODUCTION

The purpose of this report is to provide information for the management of Zealous Corporation about an increasingly popular form of financing: convertible debt. Convertible debt is an issue of debt securities (bonds) that carry the option of exchange for equity securities (usually common stock).

The primary focus of the report is the accounting requirements for convertible debt and the reasons for those requirements.

Four major topics make up the report: (1) Nature of Convertible Bonds, (2) Financial Advantages and Disadvantages, (3) Accounting Treatment, and (4) Logic of the Accounting Requirements.

SUMMARY

Zealous Corporation may benefit from convertible debt because this form of financing would enable the firm to obtain low-cost funds now, while increasing equity in the future. However, Zealous's managers should be aware of the hardships that may arise from conversion or from nonconversion; they should also be aware that accounting requirements impose a potentially unfavorable presentation of such debt in the financial statements.

1

FIGURE 9–1   Continued

NATURE OF CONVERTIBLE BONDS

When convertible bonds are issued, the bond indenture specifies a period of time after issuance during which the bonds may be converted. The indenture also specifies a conversion price, "the amount of par value of principal amount of the bonds exchangeable for one share of stock" [Bogen, 1968, p. 31]. If a conversion ratio, rather than a conversion price, is specified, the effective price of stock to the bondholder may be determined by dividing the par value of the bond by the number of shares exchangeable for one bond.

The conversion price, which is determined when the bonds are sold, is usually from 10 to 20 percent above the prevailing market price of the common stock at the time of issue. Both the issuing firm and the investor expect that the market price of the stock will rise above the conversion price, and that the conversion privilege will then be exercised by most or all bondholders.

The indenture typically includes a call provision so that the issuing firm can force bondholders to convert. Therefore, it is evident that firms issuing convertible debt often truly want to raise equity capital. The reasons that they choose convertible debt are discussed below.

FINANCIAL ADVANTAGES AND DISADVANTAGES

Advantages

The use of convertible debt has advantages over straight debt or stock issues.

FIGURE 9-1 Continued

Bonds that are convertible into stock, even if the quality of the bond is not very high, are in demand. Therefore, bond buyers are willing to accept a low stated interest rate on such bonds, to pay a premium and accept a lower yield, or to accept less restrictive covenants. The issuing firm thus obtains funds at a lower cost than would be possible if the firm issued bonds without the conversion privilege.

The advantages of a convertible bond issue over a common stock issue relate to timing. The firm is willing to take on more equity in the future, but is reluctant to sell stock under present conditions. For example, if the price of the firm's stock is temporarily depressed,

> to sell stock now would require giving up more shares to raise a given amount of money than management thinks is necessary. However, setting the conversion price 10 to 20 percent above the present market price of the stock will require giving up 10 to 20 percent fewer shares when the bonds are converted than would be required if stock were sold directly [Brigham, 1978, p. 532].

Another possible advantage of convertibles, related to the number of shares given up, is the retention of certain ownership interests. For example, one stockholder may own most of the stock and want to maintain control. He or she may be able to do so by voting against a large issue of stock, advocating instead the issue of bonds which are convertible into a number of shares small enough not to injure the stockholder's majority.

FIGURE 9-1 Continued

Disadvantages

Most of the disadvantages of convertibles are related to the uncertainty of the conversion and its timing. If the stock price does not rise, conversion will not occur, and the issuing firm will not obtain the equity financing it desired. The firm might then have difficulty meeting the unplanned-for obligations of debt. On the other hand, if the price of the common stock increases, the issuing firm might have been better off to wait and sell the common stock.

Other disadvantages arise when the conversion occurs. When the debt becomes equity, earnings per share is reduced, operating leverage is reduced, and income taxes rise because interest expense is reduced.

ACCOUNTING TREATMENT

The Accounting Principles Board, in its Opinion No. 14, ruled that convertible bonds "which are sold at a price or have a value at issuance not significantly in excess of the face amount" must be treated in the same manner as other bonds [1969, par. 1]. That is, "no portion of the proceeds from the issuance . . . should be accounted for as attributable to the conversion feature" [par. 10]. The expectation that some or all of the bonds will be converted into stock is given no recognition in the accounts.

Since convertibles are normally sold at a premium, the amount of the cash proceeds from the issue is greater than the face value of the bonds. The difference between the debit to Cash and the credit to Bonds Payable is credited to a Premium on Bonds account. The premium is amortized, using the effective interest method, over the life of the bonds.

FIGURE 9-1   Continued

5

The effect of the amortization is that the interest expense recorded by the firm each period does not equal the amount of the interest payment, but reflects the effective yield to the bondholders.

When the bonds are converted, the firm removes from the accounts the balances associated with those bonds: Bonds Payable is debited for the par value of the bonds converted, and the Premium account is debited for the portion of the unamortized premium which is attributable to the bonds converted. Two methods can be used to record the common stock issued in exchange for the bonds. Under one method, the stock is assigned a value equal to the market value of the stock or the bonds. If this value differs from the book value of the bonds (the balances associated with the bonds, mentioned above), then a gain or a loss is recorded. Under the other method, which is more widely used, the value assigned to the stock equals the book value of the bonds, and no gain or loss is recognized or recorded [Kieso and Weygandt, 1986, pp. 695–96].

If the issuing firm retires its convertible bonds for cash before their maturity date, the transaction is recorded in the same way as the early retirement of any other debt. The difference between the book value of the bonds and the cash paid to retire them is a gain or a loss. If the gain or loss is material, it is shown as an extraordinary item on the income statement.

While convertibles are accounted for solely as debt, accountants must consider the equity characteristics of such issues in computing earnings per share (EPS). APB Opinion No. 15 requires that corporations which have issued securities that are potentially dilutive of EPS must

FIGURE 9-1 Continued

152

present, in their financial statements, two EPS figures. If a convertible security meets the requirements of certain tests, as outlined in SFAS No. 55, it is considered a common stock equivalent and enters the calculation of primary EPS; otherwise, it enters only the calculation of fully diluted EPS [Kieso and Weygandt, 1986, pp. 716-17].

Both EPS figures represent EPS as if the bonds had been converted into stock. If they had been converted, the removal of the bonds would have caused a reduction of interest expense, which would have increased earnings; therefore, the accountant revises the earnings, as well as the number of shares, upward [Kieso and Weygandt, 1986 pp. 717-19]. However, the positive effect of the earnings adjustment may not offset the negative effect of the shares adjustment. The result is that convertibles reduce reported EPS.

LOGIC OF THE ACCOUNTING REQUIREMENTS

In requiring that convertible debt be accounted for solely as debt, the APB reasoned that the debt and the conversion feature are inseparable [Opinion 14, 1969, par. 10]. That is, at any given time, a security is either all debt or all equity. Therefore, since at the time of issuance the security is all debt, its issuance should be recorded as debt.

The Board argued further that practical problems exist in the attempt to value the debt and conversion features separately. The conversion feature is difficult to value because of the uncertainty of the timing of conversion, and because of the uncertain future market value

FIGURE 9-1 Continued

of the stock. The debt part of the security is difficult to value independently of the conversion option, because the conversion option affects the terms of the bond. An attempt to value the bonds as if they were not convertible would require the assumption of higher terms—an unrealistic assumption, because the issuing firm would not have wanted to issue bonds with those terms [Opinion 14, 1969, par. 6].

The accounting requirements concerning presentation of EPS are intended to meet investors' reporting needs. In its Opinion No. 15, the APB explains that the value of a convertible security "is derived in large part from the value of the common stock to which it is related," and that the holder of such a security is essentially a participator in "the earnings and earnings potential of the issuing corporation" [1969, par. 25]. Therefore, the determination of EPS based only on outstanding shares of common stock "would place form over substance" [par. 26], and would mislead the investors.

CONCLUSION

In the decision whether to finance with convertible debt, Zealous must consider whether its situation would benefit from using convertibles rather than straight debt or stock issues, and whether it can meet the debt requirements, should conversion not occur as expected. In addition, management should analyze carefully the effect of the issue on readers of the financial statements, because until the bonds are converted, a possibly high level of debt will exist alongside a lowered presentation of earnings per share.

FIGURE 9-1 Continued

8

WORKS CITED

Accounting Principles Board, <u>Accounting for Convertible Debt and Debt
Issued with Stock Purchase Warrants</u>, Opinion No. 14 (N.Y.: AICPA,
1969).

Accounting Principles Board, <u>Earnings per Share</u>, Opinion No. 15 (N.Y.:
AICPA, 1969).

Bogen, J.I., ed., <u>Financial Handbook</u>, 4th ed. (N.Y.: Ronald Press,
1968).

Booker, J.A., and Jarnagin, B.D., <u>Financial Accounting Standards:
Explanation and Analysis</u> (Chicago: Commerce Clearing House, 1979).

Brigham, E.F., <u>Fundamentals of Financial Management</u>, (Hinsdale, Ill.:
Dryden Press, 1978).

Financial Accounting Standards Board, <u>Determining Whether a Convertible
Security Is a Common Stock Equivalent</u>, Statement of Financial
Accounting Standards No. 55 (Stamford, Conn.: FASB, 1982).

Kieso, D.E., and Weygandt, J.J., <u>Intermediate Accounting</u>, 5th ed.,
(N.Y.: Wiley, 1986).

FIGURE 9-1 Continued

of income from the sale of development properties. While there is considerable variation within the association, a typical contract has a down payment of 5 to 15 percent. Remaining payments may be spread over many years.

The managing partner of your firm has asked you to write a report on recognition of income from land development sales. This report will be distributed to the real estate developers who make up Southeastern Enterprises.[4]

Exercise 9–4
(Intermediate or Auditing)

Write a report in response to the letter on page 157[5] (Figure 9–2).

Exercise 9–5
(Intermediate or Auditing)

Write a report in response to the letter on page 159[6] (Figure 9–3).

Exercise 9–6
(Auditing)

The Lakeland Milk Products Company is a medium-sized company engaged in purchasing unpasteurized milk and processing it into different dairy products. For the past six years Lakeland has had services performed by a CPA firm, which includes audit services, tax services, and management consulting services. Since Lakeland lacks a competent controller, a major part of the fee has consisted of correcting the accounting records, making adjusting entries, and preparing the annual financial statements. Recently, the president of Lakeland asked the CPA in charge of the Lakeland audit for the past three years if he would be interested in becoming the full-time combination controller and internal auditor for the company.

1. Which services currently being provided by the CPA firm could be done by the CPA acting in his new capacity, assuming he is qualified to perform them?
2. Which services must the CPA firm continue to perform, even if the new controller is qualified? Why must they be done by the CPA firm?
3. Explain specific ways the controller can help reduce the CPA's audit fee if he is knowledgeable about the way the audit is conducted.[7]

Prepare your answer in the form of a report to the president of Lakeland.

Exercise 9–7
(Accounting Information Systems)

Select a small business in your community that plans to improve its accounting system. Analyze the business's needs for an accounting system, including the possibility of a microcomputer.

```
                                    Office of the Controller
                                    Southern Cement
                                    1021 Peachtree Ave.
                                    Atlanta, GA   30309

                                    January 10, 1989


Mary L. De Quincy
Auditor-in-Charge
Lewis and Clark, C.P.A.s
111 Baxter St.
Athens, GA   30605

Dear Ms. De Quincy:

     Last year's fiscal year will be the fifteenth year that you have
audited our financial statements.  I appreciate the work you have done
for us.

     As you know, the company has been growing steadily since our in-
ception 75 years ago.  The last 10 years have been particularly good
because of Atlanta's tremendous growth in condominiums.  Continued growth
has required us to purchase at a rapid rate machinery to mix and pour
cement at construction sites.  Almost all of our machinery has been
financed by Confederate National Bank.  Until now, the bank has been
eager to lend us money at the prime rate when using the machines as
collateral.

     Southern Cement usually makes large down payments from contract
proceeds on equipment purchases.  Lately we have experienced equipment
purchasing problems because our contracts do not require payment until
the contract is complete.  We have recently accepted some long-term
contracts that will be quite lucrative, but we will not receive payment
for two years.  There is no reason to believe that we will not be paid
eventually.

     Confederate National refuses to make additional equipment loans
to us because it believes we are "over-leveraged."  The loan officer
supports this refusal by calling attention to our debt-to-equity ratio,
which is higher than those of our competitors.

     Southern Cement's liabilities are higher than the liabilities of
our competitors due to one account -- deferred taxes.  The deferred
taxes account is higher for Southern Cement for two reasons:

     (1)  Our company is older than the competitors and deferred taxes
          have accumulated over a number of years.

     (2)  Tax advantages from accelerated depreciation on equipment pur-
          chases in the last 10 years have allowed us to defer large
          amounts of tax payments.
```

FIGURE 9-2   Letter for Exercise 9-4.

Mary L. De Quincy
January 10, 1989
Page 2

    I do not anticipate this account to decline in the future since
our company continues to require additional equipment. Quite frankly,
I have never seen the need to include deferred taxes in the liability
section of the balance sheet since it is highly unlikely that these
amounts will ever be paid to the federal government. Deferred taxes
that become due have always been replaced by a greater amount that will
be deferred. The deferred tax account has continued to grow at a steady
rate. Removal of deferred taxes that will not become due would significantly reduce Southern Cement's debt-to-equity ratio enough to convince
any banker to make an additional equipment loan to us.

    In the last three years, several other CPA firms have approached
me to solicit our account. Out of curiosity I recently asked one of
them whether it would be possible to issue an unqualified opinion on
a balance sheet prepared without deferred taxes as a liability. A member
of one firm claimed that he saw no problems; however, his firm would
require an additional fee to cover research costs in financial statement
preparation. Since I am reluctant to change accountants, is it possible
for you to prepare the financial statements without including deferred
taxes? The absence of deferred taxes would provide the following advantages.

    (1) Eliminate a "false liability" which misleads our creditors
         and stockholders.

    (2) Reduce our debt-to-equity ratio, thereby allowing us to obtain
         our desperately needed loan.

    I have never fully understood the disclosure requirements for de-
ferred taxes. I do believe, however, that the elimination of this account from our balance sheet would result in a more accurate represen-
tation of our financial position. I would appreciate a detailed analysis
of your position on this proposal.

                                    Sincerely,

                                    Sandy Loam
                                    Sandy Loam
                                    Controller

FIGURE 9-2   Continued

Office of the Controller
Internal Furnishings, Inc.
Dallas, Texas 77840

September 30, 1989

B.B. May
Auditor-in-Charge
External Accounting Partners
Dallas, Texas 77841

Dear B.B.:

It has been almost a year since you helped us set up a noncontributory
defined benefit pension program for our employees. You are aware that
our company has been moderately profitable in the past few years and
we do not anticipate this trend to change in the next five years (a
trend that should provide adequate funds for the pension plan). While
we are all excited about the prospects of retiring rich, there have
been some problems with the implementation of the pension system and
the recording of pension transactions. As consultant to our pension
plan project, you may be able to help us by addressing the following:

(1) I am unclear about the role of the actuary in the pension plan
process. Could you please describe what an actuary is and what tasks
we should expect an actuary to perform in our pension plan? You also
mentioned that actuarial gains and losses can occur in pension accounting. Please describe how these gains and losses occur and the different
methods we can use to account for these costs.

(2) You probably remember that we allocated $500,000 for five years
of past service cost. You explained to me that normal cost liabilities
relate to qualified employee service after the inception of the plan
and past service costs relate to qualified employee services before
the inception of the plan. I suggest that in order to abide by the
matching concept we expense normal pension cost after the pension inception date and expense past service costs before the inception date.
Past service costs could be deducted (debited) from retained earnings.
If this is in violation of generally accepted accounting principles,
please let me know the correct procedure and why it is better than my
way.

FIGURE 9-3   Letter for Exercise 9-5.

B.B. May
September 30, 1989
Page 2

(3) I read that a pension expense must be between maximum and minimum limits. These limits do not seem difficult to calculate; however, I am curious about why they exist. Would you please explain to me in simple terms the purpose of maximum and minimum limits and how they were developed?

Thank you for your help.

Sincerely,

Art Deco

Art Deco
Controller

FIGURE 9-3   Continued

This project will probably require you to interview the business's management so that you understand how the business operates, what its systems needs are, and the budgetary constraints within which management will be working.

You may decide, after evaluating the business's needs, that it does not need a microcomputer at the present time. If this is the case, write a five- or ten-year systems plan based on projected growth of the business.

If you do conclude that the business should purchase a microcomputer, what hardware and software do you recommend?

If the business already has a computer system, should it scrap the present system or update it?

Write your evaluation and recommendation in the form of a report to the business's manager or owner.

NOTES

1. Jean Bryan, "Financial and Accounting Considerations of Issuing Convertible Debt" (unpublished student paper, University of Georgia, 1980).
2. Gordon S. May, "Writing Assignment for Intermediate Accounting" (unpublished class assignment, University of Georgia, 1982).
3. Randolph A. Shockley, "Writing Assignment for Intermediate Accounting" (unpublished class assignment, University of Georgia, 1982).
4. Roger A. Roemmich, "Writing Assignment for Intermediate Accounting" (unpublished class assignment, University of Georgia, 1982).
5. William R. Pasewark, "Writing Assignment for Intermediate Accounting" (unpublished class assignment, University of Georgia, 1986).
6. Ibid.
7. Alvin A. Arens and James K. Loebbecke, *Auditing: An Integrated Approach,* 2nd ed. (Englewood Cliffs, N.J.: Prentice-Hall, Inc., © 1980), p. 73. Reprinted by permission.

CHAPTER 10
Essays: An Approach to Organization and Development

A chapter entitled "Essays" might sound too academic for a writing handbook for accountants. The chapter is included here, however, for two reasons. First, many undergraduate and graduate students take exams with essay questions, and they may need guidance in answering these questions effectively. Second, many of the basic principles of organizing and developing an essay are applicable to memos, reports, and other types of writing used by accountants in practice.

This chapter begins with a brief section on short discussion questions, followed by a closer look at the organization and development of a longer essay.

SHORT DISCUSSION QUESTIONS

The key to answering a one- or two-paragraph discussion question is well-organized paragraphs with strong topic sentences (see Chapter 3). Sometimes the question itself will suggest the topic sentence. For example, consider the question:

Discuss who the users of financial statements are.

The answer to this question might begin with the following sentence:

The users of an organization's financial statements are mainly external to the organization.

The first paragraph of the answer would discuss external users—investors, creditors, government agencies, etc. A second, shorter paragraph might then discuss internal users of financial statements—management, employees, etc. The second topic sentence might be as follows:

> People within an organization are also interested in its financial statements.

ESSAYS

Before you read this section, go back and review the section in Chapter 3 on paragraph development; pay particular attention to the complex-deductive pattern of organization.

Complex-deductive paragraphs have a main idea (topic sentence) supported by major and minor supports. Essays—discussions of four or more paragraphs— are organized the same way, except that the main idea (thesis statement) has as its major supports paragraphs rather than sentences. In addition, the thesis statement usually comes at the end of the first paragraph; it is preceded by attention-getting sentences. Here is the basic outline of a five-paragraph essay:

I. Introduction—first paragraph
   A. Attention-getting sentences
   B. Thesis statement—main idea of the essay, usually expressed in one sentence
II. Body of the essay—develops the thesis through analysis, explanation, examples, proofs, or steps
   A. Major support—second paragraph
      1.
      2.   Minor supports—sentences which develop the paragraph in a simple- or complex-deductive organization
      3. etc.
   B. Major support—third paragraph
      1.
      2.   minor supports
      3.
   C. Major support—fourth paragraph
      1.
      2.   minor supports
      3.
III. Conclusion—fifth paragraph
   A. Repeats the essay's main idea—a variation of the thesis statement
   B. Forceful ending

Some of the parts of this outline need more discussion.

Attention-getting Sentences

The purpose of the attention-getting sentences is to get the reader interested in the subject. Several techniques can be used:

- Give background information about the topic. Why is the topic of current interest?
- Pose a problem or raise a question (to be answered in the essay).
- Define key terms, perhaps the topic itself.
- Show the relevance of the topic to the reader.
- Begin with an interesting direct quotation.
- Relate a brief anecdote relevant to the topic.
- Relate the specific topic to a wider area of interest.

The following essay introduction uses two of these techniques. It poses a question and then suggests the relevance of the topic to the reader, if we assume that the essay was written for an audience of accountants. The final sentence of the paragraph is the thesis statement.

> Do accountants need to be good writers? Some people would answer "No" to this question. They believe an accountant's job is limited to arithmetical calculations with very little need to use words or sentences. But this picture of an accountant's responsibilities is a misconception. In fact, good writing skills are essential to the successful practice of accounting.

Notice how smoothly the attention-getting sentences flow into the thesis statement. Be careful that there is not an abrupt jump in these two parts of the introduction. You may need to use a transition such as the one in the above paragraph ("In fact, . . .").

Thesis Statement

The thesis statement summarizes the main idea of the essay, usually in one sentence. It may be a *simple* thesis statement, such as the one just studied. Alternatively, the thesis statement may be *expanded*. That is, it may summarize the main supports of the discussion. Here is an example of an expanded thesis statement:

> In fact, successful accountants must have good writing skills to communicate with clients, managers, agencies, and colleagues.

Sometimes, to avoid a long or awkward sentence, you may want to use two sentences for the thesis statement.

> In fact, good writing skills are essential to the successful practice of accounting. For example, during a typical business day an accountant may write to clients, managers, agencies, or colleagues.

Conclusion

The conclusion must do at least one thing: repeat the discussion's main idea, usually in some variation of the thesis statement. In addition, effective conclusions often end with a forceful statement that will stay in the reader's mind, thus giving the discussion a more lasting impact. For a strong ending you can use several techniques, many of which resemble those used in the introduction.

- Show a broad application of the ideas suggested in the discussion.
- End with an authoritative direct quotation that reinforces your position.
- Challenge the reader.
- Echo the attention-getting sentences. For example, if you began by posing a question in the introduction, you can answer it explicitly in the conclusion.

Applying Essay Techniques to Other Kinds of Writing

If you are answering an essay question on an exam, you can use the techniques just discussed to organize and develop an effective discussion. But how do these techniques work with the writing formats more typically used by accountants—letters, memos, and reports?

First of all, as we have seen in earlier chapters, everything you write should have a main idea. In an essay this idea is called the thesis statement; in a memo or report the main idea might be included in the statement of purpose. But whatever you're writing, it is a good idea to identify the main idea before you even begin your outline. Unless this idea is clear in your mind—or clearly written in your notes—what you write may be rambling and confusing. Your reader might then wonder, "What's this person trying to say? What's the point?"

So whatever you write should be organized around a central idea, just as an essay is organized. Letters, reports, and memos share other features of an essay as well: a basic three-part structure (introduction, body, conclusion); complex-deductive organization; and the need for adequate transitions and concrete support.

If you understand the principles discussed in this chapter, you will have an easier job planning and organizing the writing tasks which are part of your professional responsibilities.

SAMPLE ESSAY

Below is an actual assignment for an essay in an intermediate accounting class. Following the assignment is a student's answer that illustrates some of the principles of good organization and development.

Assignment[1]

A small company has just hired you to replace its bookkeeper, who left for Barbados with a sales manager. Before the bookkeeper resigned, she explained the accounting system to the company president. In his 15-minute review of the system, the president learned his company had a general journal, four special journals, a general ledger, and two subsidiary ledgers.

His first suggestion to you is that you cut costs and reduce duplication of effort. He suggests that you use only one journal instead of five and does not see any need for ledgers since they only duplicate what is already recorded in the journal.

Explain in 300–500 words how the president's suggestions may increase rather than reduce costs, and require more rather than less effort.

Essay[2]

Good accounting, like good management, relies on an organized system and a division of labor to reduce costs and minimize effort. Multiple journals and ledgers actually save the company time and money by isolating related accounts, delegating details, and summarizing information in controlling accounts. Isolation, delegation, and summarization free the accountant from the time-consuming task of sorting through overcrowded controlling accounts, thereby minimizing effort and reducing cost.

Isolation of accounts into special journals and subsidiary ledgers allows the accountant or manager to collect information on specific accounts in a small amount of time. Special journals, categorized as cash receipts, sales on account, purchases on account, and payments of cash, isolate each of these activities. Data can be reviewed for timely managerial decisions at a moment's notice because special journals eliminate the need to sort through other transactions. Likewise, subsidiary ledgers keep a running total of balances in a related category. The information remains separate and easily accessible and therefore of greatest use not only to the accountant, but also to management.

Delegation of transactions into special and subsidiary records eliminates clutter in controlling accounts and also allows for ease of data collection. For example, Herb Company has 2,000 customers and over 50 creditors. The accountant uses subsidiary ledgers to organize these accounts into visible information. If a creditor double-bills the company, a quick check of that ledger will reveal the problem. Searching through a cluttered control account for the same information would prove tedious and leave room for error. Although the use of subsidiary ledgers does require double posting, the initial expenditure of time more than repays itself in time and money saved. Those 2,000 customers and over 50 creditors need room in subsidiary ledgers to free control accounts for other important transactions.

Finally, summarization of subsidiary and special records occurs in the controlling accounts, providing the accountant and management with an overall view of the company's transactions. Interested parties "get the big picture" without seeing all of the transactions at once because all account totals are posted to control accounts.

Cost reduction and labor savings result from the isolation, delegation, and summarization processes. Although account cutbacks may seem at first to provide an easy solution, after closer inspection the true picture emerges. Control accounts, supported by additional journals and ledgers, actually save time because of their unique organization, and that saves money.

EXERCISES

Discuss the topics defined in the following exercises, using the techniques covered in this and earlier chapters. Your answer might range from one to five paragraphs or more, depending on the topic.

Exercise 10-1
(Intermediate)

Contrast financial and managerial accounting.

Exercise 10-2
(Intermediate)

Define and discuss depreciation as used in accounting.

Exercise 10-3
(Intermediate)

The following are samples of the interpretation and remarks that are frequently encountered with regard to financial statements. Do you agree or disagree with these observations? Explain fully.

1. "Sales show the cash coming in from customers, and the various expenses show the cash going out for goods and services. The difference is net income."
2. "Why can't that big steel company pay higher wages and dividends too? It can use its hundreds of millions of dollars of retained income to do so."
3. "The total stockholders' equity measures the amount that the shareholders would get today if the corporation were liquidated."[3]

Exercise 10-4
(Intermediate)

Discuss why intraperiod tax allocation is necessary.

Exercise 10-5
(Intermediate)

Inventory may be computed under one of various cost-flow assumptions. Among these assumptions are first-in, first-out (FIFO) and last-in, first-out (LIFO). In the past, some companies have changed from FIFO to LIFO for computing portions, or all, of their inventory.

1. Ignoring income tax, what effect does a change from FIFO to LIFO have on net earnings and working capital? Explain.

2. Explain the difference between the FIFO assumption of earnings and operating cycle and the LIFO assumption of earnings and operating cycle.*

Exercise 10-6
(Intermediate)

Generally accepted accounting principles require the use of accruals and deferrals in the determination of income.

1. How does accrual accounting affect the determination of income? Include in your discussion what constitutes an accrual and a deferral, and give appropriate examples of each.
2. Contrast accrual accounting with cash accounting.**

Exercise 10-7
(Intermediate)

The Financial Accounting Standards Board issued its Statement Number 12 to clarify accounting methods and procedures with respect to certain marketable securities. An important part of the statement concerns the distinction between noncurrent and current classification of marketable securities.

1. Why does a company maintain an investment portfolio of current and noncurrent securities?
2. What factors should be considered in determining whether investments in marketable equity securities should be classified as current or noncurrent, and how do these factors affect the accounting treatment for unrealized losses? †

Exercise 10-8
(Intermediate)

Financial accounting usually emphasizes the economic substance of events even though the legal form may differ and suggest different treatment. For example, under accrual accounting, expenses are recognized when they are incurred (substance) rather than when cash is disbursed (form).

Although the feature of substance over form exists in most generally accepted accounting principles and practices, there are times when form prevails over substance.

For each of the following topics, discuss the underlying theory in terms of both substance and form, that is, substance over form and possibly form over substance in some cases. Each topic should be discussed independently.

*Material from Uniform CPA Examinations and Unofficial Answers, Copyright © 1979 by the American Institute of Certified Public Accountants, Inc., is adapted with permission.

**Material from Uniform CPA Examinations and Unofficial Answers, Copyright © 1979 by the American Institute of Certified Public Accountants, Inc., is adapted with permission.

†*Material from Uniform CPA Examinations and Unofficial Answers, Copyright © 1977 by the American Institute of Certified Public Accountants, Inc., is adapted with permission.

1. Consolidated financial statements
2. Equity method of accounting for investments in common stock.
3. Leases (including sale and leaseback).
4. Earnings per share (complex capital structure).*

Exercise 10–9
(Auditing)

Discuss the benefits of preparing an engagement letter.

Exercise 10–10
(Auditing)

The first generally accepted auditing standard of field work requires, in part, that "the work is to be adequately planned." An effective tool that aids the auditor in adequately planning the work is an audit program.

Answer the following question in essay form.

What is an audit program, and what purposes does it serve?**

Exercise 10–11
(Tax)

Discuss the depreciability of the following:

1. A law firm's research library.
2. The cost of excavating, grading, and removal directly associated with roadway construction.
3. A house built and occupied by a farmer and his family.
4. A farmer's lemon grove.
5. A vacant lot suitable for commercial buildings.[4]

Exercise 10–12
(All levels)

As part of a public relations campaign, the CPA firm you work for has decided to publish a series of short (500–1,000 words) brochures explaining some basic accounting concepts and procedures. Many of the firm's clients own small businesses. Although these clients are experienced in business, most have little formal accounting education.

You will need to write the brochures so that the clients can understand them. On the other hand, you do not want to "talk down" to them or sound patronizing.

Write essays on the following topics. The essays will serve as the basis of the brochures.

1. cash versus accrual accounting
2. inventory accounting
3. expense and revenue recognition
4. internal control of cash
5. accounting for inflation
6. the primary financial statements
7. regulation of the accounting professon: public versus private sector
8. accounting for leases
9. the history of the accounting profession
10. the audit

NOTES

1. William Timothy O'Keefe, "Writing Assignment for Intermediate Accounting" (unpublished class assignment, University of Georgia, 1980).
2. Sandra L. Herbelin, "Journals and Ledgers" (unpublished student paper, University of Georgia, 1980).
3. Adapted from Charles Horngren, *Introduction to Financial Accounting* (Englewood Cliffs, N.J.: Prentice-Hall, Inc., © 1981), p. 65. Reprinted by permission.
4. Prentice Hall, *1988 Federal Tax Course* (Englewood Cliffs, N.J.: Prentice-Hall, Inc., © 1987), p. 442. Reprinted by permission.

CHAPTER 11
Research Papers

Sometimes accountants need to research the professional accounting literature as one step in the preparation of a report or other document. This research may involve an in-depth look at official pronouncements, such as the Opinions of the Accounting Principles Board (APB) or Statements of the Financial Accounting Standards Board (FASB). Sometimes, too, accountants must research the details of government regulations, such as provisions of the Internal Revenue Code. And occasionally accountants need to read other kinds of professional literature, such as journal articles or monographs on topics of current interest.

This chapter discusses, in an elementary step-by-step approach, how to write a research paper. Much of the material will be review for students or professionals who have written term papers or documented reports. However, the suggestions should be helpful to anyone who must research the professional literature and then summarize the results of that research in a written form.

HOW TO START

If you are writing a paper that requires research of the literature, chances are you already know something about the topic. If you don't, or if your memory is only vague, do some initial reading so that you have a basic familiarity with your subject. An accounting textbook may be a good place to start.

Once you have a general idea of what your topic involves, you will need to look for additional information. Many times the next step will be to look at official accounting pronouncements, such as those found in *Accounting Standards: Current*

Text.[1] Or you may need to study government regulations or laws to find out how to handle a client's technical problem. For either case, read the material carefully and take accurate notes of your findings, including references to the sources you are using. A later section of this chapter discusses note taking in more detail.

Some research papers will require a search for additional source materials in the library. It is a good idea to consult a librarian to see what help is available to you. Some libraries have computer search facilities and staff who will work with you to help you find the materials you need.

One reference which you may find in the library is the *Accountant's Index,*[2] which lists articles published in accounting periodicals. The index is arranged chronologically in volumes covering perhaps half a year. Within each volume, the articles are grouped according to topic and author. Be imaginative in looking for articles on your topic; consider the different headings it could be listed under. For example, "Stock rights" might be listed as "Fractional share rights," "Share rights," or "Stock warrants."

The library will likely have other references as well that you may find helpful. For example, many newspapers, including *The Wall Street Journal,* publish an index.

The librarian can help you find these and other references that will help you prepare your paper.

NOTE TAKING

Once you have located a useful source, take notes on what you read. For this step in your research you will need two sets of cards— 3 × 5 " cards for the bibliography and 4 × 6 " (or 5 × 8 ") cards for the notes. Using these cards will save time and trouble in the long run, even though they may seem like a bother at the time you are reading. They will help you keep track of your sources and notes, and they will be easy to use when you write your draft.

Let's look first at a bibliography card.

FIGURE 11-1   Bibliography Card

(1)

Horngren, Charles T., and
Sundem, Gary L.
<u>Introduction to Financial
Accounting</u>. 3rd ed.
Englewood Cliffs, N.J.:
Prentice-Hall, Inc., 1987.

Be sure that you include on the card all the information you will need for your bibliography (see "Documentation," pages 175–178). It is frustrating to make an extra trip to the library just to check on a date or page number.

Note cards contain the information you will actually use in your paper.[3]

```
Outline ──▶   II. A. 1                    ① p. 782      ◀── Source
 code                                                        of note

Heading ──▶       Return on Sales - definition
                  " Net income divided              ◀── The note
                    by sales. "                          itself- in this
                                                         example, a direct
                                                         quotation (note
                                                         the quotation
                                                         marks).
```

FIGURE 11-2   Note Card

Notice the parts of the note card. The numbers in the upper right-hand corner give the source (from the bibliography card) and the page(s) where this information was found. The heading gives you an idea of what this note card is about. The note itself is taken from the source. It is the material you will use in your paper.

DIRECT QUOTATION AND PARAPHRASE

You can take notes in two ways, as direct quotation (the exact words from the source) or as paraphrase (your words and sentence structures). It is usually much better to take the notes in your own words. If you take the time to paraphrase as you research, you will save time when you write your draft.

Here is a good way to paraphrase. Read a section from your source—perhaps several short paragraphs. Then look away from the page and try to remember the important ideas. Write them down. Then look back at your source to check your notes for accuracy.

Occasionally you may want to use a direct quotation. When you copy a quotation on a note card, use quotation marks so you'll know later that these are someone else's words. Copy the quotation *exactly,* including capitalization and punctuation.

It is important that direct quotations be accurate and that paraphrases be your own words and sentence structures, not just a slight variation of your source.

It is also important to give credit for material you borrow from another writer. If you do not, you will be guilty of plagiarism. *The Harbrace College Handbook* contains the following discussion of plagiarism:

If you fail to acknowledge borrowed material, then you are plagiarizing. Plagiarism is literary theft. When you copy the words of another, be sure to put those words inside quotation marks and to acknowledge the source with a footnote. When you paraphrase the words of another, use your own words and your own sentence structure, and be sure to give a footnote citing the source of the idea. A plagiarist often merely changes a few words or rearranges the words of the source. As you take notes and as you write your paper, be especially careful to avoid plagiarism.[4]

The *MLA Handbook* defines plagiarism as "the act of using another person's writing without acknowledging the source."[5] The most obvious form of plagiarism is to use another person's words, but sometimes plagiarism is more subtle:

> Other forms of plagiarism include repeating someone else's particularly apt phrase without appropriate acknowledgment, paraphrasing another person's argument as your own, and presenting another's line of thinking in the development of an idea as though it were your own.[6]

The key to avoiding plagiarism, of course, is to document your sources adequately with either internal documentation or notes (see pages 175–178). In actual practice, however, there may be situations when you will not know whether you should identify the source of information you wish to use in your paper. The difficulty arises because information that is considered "common knowledge" in a given field need not be documented.

Obviously the problem is to decide what is "common knowledge." One rule of thumb says that if you can find the same information in three different sources, that information is considered common knowledge and therefore need not be documented.

There are indeed many grey areas when it comes to issues of plagiarism. Perhaps the safest rule is to document your sources whenever there is any question of possible plagiarism.

THE OUTLINE

As you are taking notes, you will probably form some idea of the major divisions of the paper. That is, you should be getting a rough idea of its outline.

Go ahead and write down your ideas for an outline. The more reading you do, the more complete the outline will become. Stop and evaluate the outline from time to time. Are you covering all the important areas of your topic? Is the outline getting too long? Should you narrow the topic? Are some sections of the outline irrelevant to the topic? Answering these questions will guide you as you continue your research.

Once your research is complete, or nearly so, you should refine your outline. Be sure that your topic is covered completely and that the ideas are arranged in the most effective order. Think about the introduction and conclusion to your paper, and any other relevant parts. For example, do you want to include charts, tables, or graphs?

Next, arrange the note cards in the order of the outline. It is a good idea to write the outline code in the upper left-hand corner of the card.

With a completed outline and an orderly stack of note cards, you are ready to write the draft.

THE DRAFT

The draft of a research paper is written just like that of any other kind of writing (see Chapter 2), with the exception that you are incorporating note cards into your own ideas. If you have already paraphrased the notes, your task is much easier.

You do need to include in your draft an indication of where your notes came from. In other words, you want to give credit for words or ideas that are not your own. In the final version of your paper, these references will be the footnotes, endnotes, or parenthetical citations. In the draft, you can indicate your sources with a parenthetical notation like this: (① p. 782). The numbers come from the note card and refer to the source and page number of the note.

REVISING

After you have completed the draft of your research paper, you will need to revise it to perfect the organization, development, style, grammar, and spelling. Review Chapter 2 for a discussion of revision.

DOCUMENTATION

Any information you get from a source other than your own knowledge must be documented; that is, you must say where you got the information. Styles for documentation vary, but we will look at two of the most common, internal documentation and notes.

Internal Documentation

Many writers prefer to use internal documentation, which places information about sources within the text, using brackets [ ] or parentheses ( ). What goes within the brackets depends on the kind of source you are using. The list on pages 176–177 gives sample citations for sources typically used by accountants. For further information on internal documentation, you can consult *The Chicago Manual of Style*[7] or the *Publication Manual of the American Psychological Association*.[8]

It is a good idea to introduce quotations or paraphrases within the text itself:

> *According to ARB 43,* current assets are "reasonably expected to be realized in cash or sold or consumed during the normal operating cycle of the business" [Ch. 3A, par. 4].

Information you include in the introduction to the quotation or paraphrase does not need to be repeated within the brackets. Thus in this example *ARB 43* was left out of the brackets, since it was mentioned in the introductory phrase.

Notice also that the end punctuation for the quotation, in this case the period, comes after the brackets.

One reminder about the use of technical sources such as this one. Consider whether the readers of your paper will be familiar with the literature cited. If they are not, it is helpful to identify the source more fully and possibly give a brief explanation of its significance.

At the end of your paper you will need a reference list that identifies fully, in alphabetical order, the sources you cited within your paper. Sample entries for this list appear below.

INTERNAL DOCUMENTATION

C = Citation within the text
R = Entry in reference list

Book

C   [Kiger, Loeb, and May, 1988, p. 224]
R   Kiger, J. E., Loeb, S. E., May, G. S., *Accounting Principles,* 2nd ed. (N.Y.: Random House, 1988).

Article in a Journal

C   [Bamber, 1987]
R   Bamber, L. S., "Unexpected Earnings, Firm Size, and Trading Volume Around Quarterly Earnings Announcements," *The Accounting Review* (July 1987), pp. 510–532.

APB Opinion

C   [Opinion 25, 1972, par. 10]
R   Accounting Principles Board, *Accounting for Stock Issued to Employees,* Opinion No. 25 (N.Y.: AICPA, 1972).

FASB—Financial Accounting Standard

C   [SFAS 5, 1975, par. 15]
R   Financial Accounting Standards Board, *Accounting for Contingencies,* Statement of Financial Accounting Standards No. 5 (Stamford, CT: FASB, 1975).

FASB—Financial Accounting Concept

C   [SFAC 1, 1978, par. 3]

R   Financial Accounting Standards Board, *Objectives of Financial Reporting by Business Enterprises,* Statement of Financial Accounting Concepts No. 1 (Stamford, CT: FASB, 1978).

Primary Source Reprinted in Current Text

C   [SFAC 1, 1978, par. 3]

R   Financial Accounting Standards Board, *Objectives of Financial Reporting by Business Enterprises,* Statement of Financial Accounting Concepts No. 1 (Stamford, CT: FASB, 1978), as reported in *Accounting Standards: Current Text* (Homewood, Ill.: Irwin, 1988).

Endnotes and Footnotes

The other style of documentation in wide use is endnotes or footnotes. The difference between these two note forms is that footnotes come at the bottom of the page where the references occur, while endnotes come at the end of the paper. Most authorities consider endnotes, which are easier to write and type, quite acceptable. If you do prefer footnotes, however, your word processor may have the ability to place footnotes on the right pages, in acceptable format. You will also need a bibliography at the end of your paper listing your sources in alphabetical order.

One widely accepted authority for note and bibliography style is Kate L. Turabian's *A Manual for Writers.*[9] You may want to consult this work as you write your papers. The list on pages 177–178 gives examples of notes and bibliographical entries for typical accounting sources.

As with internal documentation, it is often a good idea to introduce your paraphrased or quoted material.

According to a recent article in *The Wall Street Journal,* many accounting firms find the poor writing skills of their new employees a serious problem.[10]

The introduction to this paraphrase tells generally where the information came from; the note and bibliographical entry give complete information about the source.

NOTES AND BIBLIOGRAPHY

N = Endnote or footnote
B = Bibliographical entry

Book

N   [1]Donald E. Kieso and Jerry J. Weygandt, *Intermediate Accounting,* 5th ed., Santa Barbara: John Wiley & Sons, 1986, p. 173.

B   Kieso, Donald E., and Weygandt, Jerry J. *Intermediate Accounting. 5th ed.* Santa Barbara: John Wiley & Sons, 1986.

Article in a Journal

N   ²Alfred Rappaport, "The Strategic Audit," *Journal of Accountancy* 149 (June 1980): 72.

B   Rappaport, Alfred. "The Strategic Audit." *Journal of Accountancy* 149 (June 1980): pp. 71–77.

APB Opinion

N   ³Accounting Principles Board, *Disclosure of Lease Commitments by Lessees,* Opinions of the Accounting Principles Board No. 31 (New York: American Institute of Certified Public Accountants, 1973), para. 8.

B   Accounting Principles Board. *Disclosure of Lease Commitments by Lessees.* Opinions of the Accounting Principles Board No. 31. New York: American Institute of Certified Public Accountants, 1979.

FASB—Financial Accounting Standard

N   ⁴Financial Accounting Standards Board, *Disclosure of Information About Major Customers: An Amendment of FASB Statement No. 14,* Statement of Financial Accounting Standards No. 30 (Stamford, Connecticut: Financial Accounting Standards Board, 1979), para. 7.

B   Financial Accounting Standards Board. *Disclosure of Information About Major Customers: An Amendment of FASB Statement No. 14.* Statement of Financial Accounting Standards No. 30. Stamford, Connecticut: Financial Accounting Standards Board, 1979.

FASB—Financial Accounting Concept

N   ⁵Financial Accounting Standards Board, *Objectives of Financial Reporting by Business Enterprises,* Statement of Financial Accounting Concepts No. 1 (Stamford, Connecticut: Financial Accounting Standards Board, 1978), para. 33.

B   Financial Accounting Standards Board. *Objectives of Financial Reporting by Business Enterprises.* Statement of Financial Accounting Concepts No. 1. Stamford, Connecticut: Financial Accounting Standards Board, 1978.

Primary Source Quoted in Current Text

N   ⁶Financial Accounting Standards Board, *Objectives of Financial Reporting by Business Enterprises,* Statement of Financial Accounting Concepts No. 1, as reported in *Accounting Standards: Current Text* (Homewood, Ill.: Irwin, 1987), Sec. 1210.

B   Financial Accounting Standards Board. *Objectives of Financial Reporting by Business Enterprises.* Statement of Financial Accounting Concepts No. 1. As reported in *Accounting Standards: Current Text.* Homewood, Ill.: Irwin, 1988.

EXERCISE

Choose one of the following topics, and narrow it if necessary. (For example, you might select "Careers with the Internal Revenue Service" rather than "Careers in Accounting.") Write a documented research paper on your topic, using the steps discussed in this chapter.

1. History of the Accounting Profession
2. Public- versus Private-Sector Regulation of Accounting
3. Accounting for the Effects of Inflation
4. Careers in Accounting
5. Accounting for Leases
6. Accounting for Oil and Gas Exploration
7. Computers and Accounting
8. Accountants in the F.B.I.

NOTES

1. Financial Accounting Standards Board, *Accounting Standards: Current Text* (Homewood, Ill.: Irwin, 1988).
2. Jane Kubat, ed., *Accountants' Index* (New York: American Institute of Certified Public Accountants).
3. Information on note card quoted from Charles T. Horngren and Gary L. Sundem, *Introduction to Financial Accounting,* 3rd ed. (Englewood Cliffs, N.J.: Prentice-Hall, Inc., © 1987), p. 782. Reprinted by permission.
4. John C. Hodges and Mary E. Whitten, *Harbrace College Handbook,* 8th ed. (New York: Harcourt Brace Jovanovich, Inc., 1977), p. 372.
5. Joseph Gibaldi and Walter S. Achtert, *MLA Handbook for Writers of Research Papers,* 2nd ed. (N.Y.: The Modern Language Association of America, 1984), p. 20.
6. Ibid., p. 21.
7. *The Chicago Manual of Style,* 13th ed. (Chicago: University of Chicago Press, 1980).
8. *Publication Manual of the American Psychological Association,* 3rd ed. (Washington, D.C.: American Psychological Association, 1983).
9. Kate L. Turabian, *A Manual for Writers of Term Papers, Theses, and Dissertations,* 5th ed. (Chicago: The University of Chicago Press, 1987).
10. Lee Berton, "Take Heart, CPAs: Finally a Story That Doesn't Attack You as Boring," *Wall Street Journal,* May 13, 1987, p. 33.

APPENDIX
Writing for Publication

Sometimes accountants write articles for publication in professional journals such as the *Journal of Accountancy, The CPA Journal,* or *Management Accounting.* The techniques discussed in this book apply to writing articles, but you will need to consider some additional pointers when you write for publication.

Start by considering the topic of the article you wish to write. Most likely, your article will be based on some of your own experiences in practice. You might also write a position paper or essay on some controversial issue currently under discussion within the profession.

Once you have chosen a topic, visit a good library to find out what else has been published recently about that subject. This research will help you in several ways:

1. You will find out what has been published recently on your topic, so your article will not repeat what has already been done.
2. You will find out what issues or approaches are of current interest in the profession.
3. You may find references that you can use in your article to support your position. Alternatively, you may find positions taken by other people that you want to refute.

Once you have your material together and have a pretty good idea of what you want to say, you will need to consider carefully the journal to which you will submit the article. This step in preparing your article is important because it will enable you to prepare the article so that it has the best chance of acceptance for publication. Consider these questions about your targeted journal:

1. Who are the readers of the journal? What are their interests and concerns?

2. What type of articles does this journal publish? Some publications prefer articles that emphasize empirical research and statistics, while others are oriented more toward practice.

3. What format, organization, and length do the journal's editors prefer? You can learn this information either from a statement of editorial policy or by studying the articles already published.

4. What writing style do the editors prefer? Articles in professional accounting journals may be written in a serious, scholarly style or a light, conversational one. All journals, however, prefer prose that is clear, readable, and concise, a style that avoids accounting jargon as much as possible.

After you analyze the journal and plan your article, draft and revise your article according to the guidelines discussed in this book. Then when you feel reasonably satisfied with the article, ask colleagues to critique it. People who have themselves successfully published may be particularly helpful.

After all this preparation, your article should have a good chance for publication. However, remember to be prepared for the possibility that your article will be rejected by the first journal you send it to.

If your article is rejected, turn it around and send it somewhere else. Be sure, though, to revise it to suit the readers and editorial policies of the new journal.

Index